T0342422

When Insurers Go Bust

An Economic Analysis of the Role and
Design of Prudential Regulation

Guillaume Plantin

Jean-Charles Rochet

Princeton University Press
Princeton and Oxford

ISBN-13: 978-0-691-12935-8 (alk. paper)
ISBN-10: 0-691-12935-5 (alk. paper)

Library of Congress Control Number: 2006936336

A catalogue record for this book is available from the British Library

This book has been composed in Times

Typeset by T&T Productions Ltd, London

Printed on acid-free paper ∞

press.princeton.edu

Printed in the United States of America

10 9 8 7 6 5 4 3 2 1

Contents

Foreword   **vii**

Acknowledgements   **viii**

1 Introduction   **1**

2 Four Recent Cases of Financially Distressed Insurers   **4**
   2.1   Independent Insurance Company Limited   4
   2.2   Groupe des Assurances Nationales   13
   2.3   Equitable Life   17
   2.4   Europavie   25
   2.5   Why Are Insurers Subject to Prudential
        Regulation? A First Pass   27

3 The State of the Art in Prudential Regulation   **29**
   3.1   The Main Features of Prudential Systems   29
   3.2   Regulation and Ruin Theory: Controlling the
        Probability of Failure   34
   3.3   Conclusions   41

**4 Inversion of the Production Cycle and Capital
Structure of Insurance Companies**   **43**
   4.1   Inversion of the Production Cycle in
        the Insurance Industry   43
   4.2   An Analogy between Insurance Capital and
        Deductibles in Insurance Contracts   45
   4.3   The Role of Deductibles in Insurance Contracts   47
   4.4   The Role of Insurance Capital to Mitigate
        Informational Problems   50

4.5   Conclusion: The Inversion of the Production Cycle
       Creates Agency Problems That Can Be Mitigated
       by Capital Requirements for Insurance Companies   53
4.6   Appendix: Capital Requirements as
       an Incentive Device   54

**5 Absence of a Tough Claimholder in the Financial
Structure of Insurance Companies and
Incomplete Contracts   56**
5.1   Absence of a Tough Claimholder   56
5.2   Prudential Regulation and Incomplete Contracts   59
5.3   The "Representation Hypothesis"   61

6 How to Organize the Regulation of Insurance Companies 64
6.1   Simple Prudential Ratios   64
6.2   "Double Trigger"   66
6.3   An Independent but Accountable Prudential
       Authority   68
6.4   Granting Control Rights to the Industry via
       a Guarantee Fund   69
6.5   A Single Accounting Standard   71
6.6   Limiting the Scope of Prudential Regulation   72
6.7   What if This Is Not Enough?   73

7 The Role of Reinsurance   75
7.1   Organization of the Reinsurance Market   75
7.2   Reinsurance and Prudential Supervision   81

**8 How Does Insurance Regulation Fit within Other
Financial Regulations?   83**
8.1   Insurance and Financial Conglomerates   83
8.2   The Regulation of Banks and of Insurance
       Companies Are Two Different Jobs   90
8.3   Insurance and Systemic Risk   93

**9 Conclusion: Prudential Regulation as a Substitute for
Corporate Governance   97**

References   99

Foreword

This timely book is a rare, cogent analysis of the regulation of insurance companies from the point of view of economics. The topic of insurance regulation has come right to the fore in the policy debates in financial regulation, and rightly so given the pivotal role of insurance companies in the financial system as direct and indirect claimholders of banks and other leveraged institutions, as well as their long-term role in channeling savings for an aging population. And yet, the current framework for insurance regulation across the advanced economies is a patchwork of rules that have built up over years, based loosely on actuarial considerations, and which differ substantially from one jurisdiction to another without much rationale. This book sets the standard for debate in this important area. The book surveys the recent episodes of failures of insurance companies, reviews the actuarial basis for insurance regulation and its weaknesses, and proposes an economic rationale for insurance regulation based on capital as a way of mitigating moral hazard. The scholarship backing the book is impeccable, as would be expected from authors of such caliber, but the book has added authority arising from the fact that one of the authors (Plantin) also has first-hand experience as an insurance regulator. The book will be of wide interest to financial economists, and will be essential reading for policy makers in central banks and financial regulatory bodies. In time, this book will gain the status of (and be seen as a natural accompaniment to) Dewatripont and Tirole's classic on the prudential regulation of banks, and will be widely read and cited.

HYUN SONG SHIN
Professor of Economics, Princeton University

Acknowledgements

This book came out of a research project commissioned by the French Federation of Insurance Companies (FFSA). We are very grateful to Philippe Trainar for his encouragement. Guillaume Plantin has benefited from illuminating discussions with the late Alain Tosetti.

When Insurers Go Bust

1
Introduction

The insurance industries of several countries have recently experienced periods of stress related to the failure of large, sometimes well-established, insurers. We begin our analysis with a study of four such cases: Independent Insurance and Equitable Life in the United Kingdom, Groupe des Assurances Nationales (GAN) and Europavie in France. These scandals have prompted a general and fierce debate (in the press, in the academic literature, but also in the political arena) about the need to reform the complex regulatory–supervisory systems that most countries have designed. The aim of this book is to offer practical recommendations, backed by rigorous economic analysis, for the reform of the prudential regulation of insurance companies.

Insurance companies are heavily regulated within virtually every country with a well-developed financial system. Moreover, insurance regulations endow public authorities with very significant control rights over insurers' strategic and financial decisions. This is even the case in countries where laissez faire economic policies are the order of the day. The regulator intervenes in the strategy and financial management of insurance companies via three channels:

- tariff restrictions;
- entry and merger restrictions;
- prudential regulation (including insurance schemes that protect against company failures).

The first two types of intervention are rather common tools, used to regulate many other sectors, such as essential facilities. By contrast, prudential regulation is specific to financial institutions. Banks are, indeed, subject to prudential rules that are very similar to those applying to insurance companies. The rationale usually invoked for the prudential regulation of banks does not clearly apply to insurance companies, however. It is commonly asserted that banks have to be regulated because of their crucial role in issuing very *liquid* claims used as means of payment, namely deposits, while financing projects by means of *illiquid* loans. Thus banks are by nature illiquid and fragile, and subject to "runs." In addition, they finance each other via the interbank market, so that isolated runs may trigger systemic panics, likely to have important real effects on economic growth. Conversely, insurance firms are invested in more liquid and tradable assets that match their liabilities much better than bank loans match bank deposits. Moreover, the organization of the reinsurance market makes it less prone to contagion than the interbank market. Thus, firms seem less fragile, and contagion less likely. Insurance panics have not occurred, to our knowledge, in recent financial history.

So, what is special about insurance? Which achievements are out of range of free insurance markets? How could a prudential regulator do better than them? These are the main questions addressed in this book.

The book is organized as follows. Chapter 2 presents four case studies of insurance companies that went bust during the 1990s. We will draw lessons from these cases throughout the remainder of the book. Chapter 3 describes the practical organization of prudential supervision in the largest insurance markets. It also describes the risk-management tools that are most commonly used to analyze prudential supervision, and stresses what we view as the limits of these tools. Chapter 4 is our first application of modern corporate-finance theory to the insurance industry. We argue that because of the length and the inversion (this notion is explained in chapter 4) of the insurance production cycle, insurance firms are subject to severe agency problems that greatly amplify their operational risks. We show how capital requirements are an appropriate tool to discipline firms and contain these risks. Chapter 5 develops another application of corporate-finance theory to prudential regulation. We discuss the role of the allocation of control rights within firms, and the reasons why it may be desirable to grant such control rights to a supervisory authority in the case of financial institutions. Reconciling the evidence described in chapter 2 with the theory developed in chapters 4 and 5, chapter 6 develops our view of the optimal design of prudential regulation in the insurance industry, and offers concrete recommendations for the practical organization of supervision. Chapter 7 discusses the specifics of reinsurance—a crucial feature of the non-life insurance business. In chapter 8 we discuss the implications of our view of regulation for two fiercely debated issues: the supervision of financial conglomerates and the management of systemic risk. Chapter 9 concludes.

The reading of this book requires no particular prerequisites, neither in financial economics nor in insurance. Very simple models support some of our points. The important intuitions underlying them are always exposed in a nontechnical fashion.

2

Four Recent Cases of Financially Distressed Insurers

In this chapter we analyze four recent scandals, each of them caused by the quasi-failure of a large insurance company. Two of them are life-insurance companies, the third is a property/casualty insurer, and the fourth is a financial conglomerate. Two of them are young firms that started out in the late 1980s, the other two are old, well-established institutions. Two are French, two are British. We emphasize that, in spite of this apparent diversity, these four cases have several salient features in common. Our aim is to shed light on these features. They are the stylized facts upon which our analysis of prudential regulation builds.

2.1 Independent Insurance Company Limited

Independent Insurance Company Limited (henceforth referred to simply as "Independent") was founded in 1987 by Michael Bright. It is a general insurance company, accepting property/casualty business mainly from British brokers. From its incorporation until 2000, Independent had all the characteristics of an insurance success story with uninterrupted profitable growth. As stated in the Director's Report for the financial year 1999 (p. 3):

The results for the year represent a thirteenth successful year with a continuation of net earned premium growth and carefully controlled underwriting.

Michael Bright was granted the British insurance achievement award in 1999. Independent received the underwriter of the year award in 1998 and the general insurer of the year award in 1999. The performance of Independent was all the more impressive because it took place in the soft insurance market of the 1990s, when most of its competitors had a hard time developing profitable new business. In addition, it is generally acknowledged among practitioners that risks accepted from brokers, as opposed to those underwritten through proprietary distribution channels, are the most difficult to control. As a result, until 2000, as summarized in *The Economist*:

City analysts tipped Independent Insurance's shares and ratings agencies gave the company a thumbs-up.

"The demise of Independent Insurance"
(June 21, 2001, www.economist.com)

On June 18, 2001, however, provisional liquidators were appointed, shortly after Independent had decided to suspend underwriting new business following discussions with the British Financial Services Authority (FSA). The magnitude of its bankruptcy is still unknown today. Estimates of the negative net wealth released by the press at the time were between 20% and 70% of liabilities (estimated to be around £1.4 billion).

How is such a rise and fall possible? Of course, the brutal collapses of Enron and WorldCom have since dwarfed this case. But those firms were operating in industries such as energy brokerage and telecommunications, with very uncertain prospects due to recent technological and organizational innovations. This is not the case for the British general insurance market, an old, very mature industry. Independent was selling classical products. Its announced business model was not revolutionary. Instead, it relied on the good old-fashioned recipe of careful underwriting, which was summarized in the 1998 Chairman's Statement (p. 3):

> The quality of underwriting continues to be one of the Company's main drivers. We refuse to compete for unprofitable business and continue to ensure that this principle pervades our whole organizational structure.

Moreover, Independent, because it is a financial institution, was closely monitored. Not only were its accounts certified by an auditing company, but its claims estimates were assessed by an appointed actuary. Furthermore, it was of course regulated by the FSA.

One reason why Independent, a firm operating in a stable, mature industry with little technological innovation, collapsed in such an unexpected fashion is the so-called "inversion of the production cycle" described in most insurance textbooks. Unlike nonfinancial firms, insurance companies sell their products—and pocket insurance premiums—a very long time before producing them, that is, before settling claims. We will elaborate further on this crucial feature of the insurance industry in the rest of the book. At this stage, it is sufficient to point out its main consequence. If Independent had operated in a business with a normal production cycle, it would probably have started experiencing operational losses by the mid 1990s or even earlier. These losses would have had to be refinanced. But before throwing any fresh money into the firm, financiers (shareholders, bondholders, and/or banks) would have made sure that the firm was properly restructured and its operations made profitable again. But here, because of the inverted production cycle, Independent continued to underwrite unprofitable business for several years. This did not lead to any liquidity problems at the time because the losses did not materialize until later. As a result, insolvency also occurred later, but on a much larger scale.

Table 2.1. Evolution of gross written premiums.

Year	95/94	96/95	97/96	98/97	99/98
Increase	39%	1%	28%	−22%	10%

The inversion of the production cycle, however, is not enough to explain this sudden collapse. Again, Independent was monitored on an ongoing basis by several institutions, exploiting detailed information processed by well-trained professionals. It is hard to believe that these institutions had no idea about Independent's difficulties in the years before its collapse. Indeed, it was not difficult to make such a guess. In the following analysis, we use only the reports and accounts of Independent as available to the public from Companies House for the period 1995–99. Quantitative information is roughly limited to the profit and loss statement and the balance sheet of the company. Let us first look at the evolution of gross written premiums over the period (see table 2.1).

Note first that such large variations are uncommon for a company with an already significant portfolio of £300 million at the end of 1994. A very interesting figure is the sharply decreasing volume during 1998. This is justified as follows in the 1998 Chairman's Statement (p. 3):

> Enormous effort was required during the year to reverse recently identified poor standards of administration and premium collection back to the levels expected of us. Partly as a result of this exercise it became evident that there was a need to re-emphasize technical disciplines throughout the London underwriting and claims functions. This resulted in reduction in premiums written during the first nine months, together with changes in personnel and the number of agents with whom we transact business.

Table 2.2.   Runoff of outstanding claims (millions of pounds).

Year	1994	1995	1996	1997	1998	1999
Amount	−0.3	2.3	−3.4	1.4	−2.1	−2.7

So, Independent acknowledged in 1998 that part of the business underwritten in the past turned out to be more costly than expected. But then, this should have led to a substantial increase in the provisions[1] for future claims. In the insurance jargon, the runoff[2] should have been negative—however, it was not significantly (see table 2.2).

Table 2.2 can be read as follows. The −2.1 in 1998 is the difference between the company's estimate of the residual value of the claims made before December 31, 1997 on the one hand, and the reevaluation of these same claims one year later on December 31, 1998 on the other. Thus, the company's estimate of the cost of claims occurred before 1997 was slightly more pessimistic in 1998 than in 1997 since it increased by £2.1 million. These amounts are not significant in a £1 billion balance sheet. Apparently, Independent did not significantly revise its reserving policy in 1998. But acknowledging that some risks were mispriced and shrinking the portfolio without reevaluating outstanding claims at the same time hardly seems consistent.

It is also interesting to note that written premiums increased significantly again in 1999 (10%). No Chairman's Statement to comment on this is disclosed in the Companies House records for 1999.

---

[1] Provisions are reserves for claims made but not settled in the European insurance terminology.

[2] The runoff is the profit or loss resulting from a reevaluation of outstanding claims. If the company has been overly optimistic in the past, provisions increase, and the runoff is said to be negative.

Table 2.3. Evolution of the profit and loss
account of Independent.

Year	1994	1995	1996	1997	1998	1999
Claims paid	29%	31%	42%	47%	59%	64%
Change in the provisions	24%	27%	13%	15%	−3%	−9%
Net ceded claims	−22%	−16%	−14%	−1%	−2%	−2%
Operations expenses	23%	23%	27%	31%	39%	36%
Total	54%	66%	69%	92%	92%	88%

Let us now take a look at the profit and loss account of the company over the period. All the figures are expressed as a percentage of the earned premiums for the year in question (see table 2.3).

Claims paid are, roughly speaking, the cash paid out by the company to settle claims. As a percentage of the premiums, it doubles over the period shown. At the same time, the change in provisions decreases sharply to become negative. This occurs in companies which do not underwrite a lot of new business and only manage the runoff of an old portfolio. As time elapses, the reserves are liquidated to settle claims. This was clearly not the case for Independent, whose activity only started declining in 1998.

On the whole, the increase in claims and the decrease in provisions offset each other so that the total (present plus future) cost of claims looks roughly stable in terms of premiums. This has two possible interpretations. An optimistic one is that Independent settled claims more quickly over the period. The production cycle was getting increasingly short and premiums spent less and less time in the balance sheet before being transformed into settled claims. A pessimistic one is that "bad" risks started to develop, so that more and more claims had to be paid. In order to maintain a balance sheet that looked good, the company financed these additional claims with a more aggressive estimation of the claims, which, of course, remained to be paid. In other words, either the same amount of claims was paid at a faster pace, or more claims had to be paid, and the evolution of the provisions was an attempt to conceal this. It is not possible to find the correct interpretation without further information. But the evolution was so dramatic, in 1996 for instance, that on-site investigations carried out by competent analysts in 1997 should have delivered the answer.

Net ceded claims are the claims paid by reinsurers (insurers of insurance companies) minus reinsurance premiums. While Independent was a profitable client for its reinsurers at the beginning of the period, it stopped being a particularly interesting one from 1997 on. This has to be interpreted very cautiously, because six years is a very small sample for reinsurance transactions. Indeed, reinsurance involves the riskiest, and hence the most volatile, part of the claims. But it seemed that the remuneration of reinsurers was on a negative trend. This was not a good signal. Indeed, a healthy insurance company makes sure its reinsurance treaties are a sufficiently good deal for reinsurers. It ensures these reinsurers are reliable long-term partners, providing liquidity quickly whenever rare catastrophic events occur.

On the whole, operations expenses (roughly speaking, administrative costs) and claims paid increased so sharply that the reduction in provisions charges and a more profitable reinsurance account did not prevent the total drifting from 54% of the premiums in 1994 to 88% in 1999.

Finally, let us examine Independent's balance sheet. The main assets used by Independent to cover future insurance claims ("technical provisions," in the insurance jargon) are

Table 2.4. Evolution of Independent's balance sheet.

Year	1994	1995	1996	1997	1998	1999
Investments	84%	89%	92%	65%	56%	42%
Reinsurers' share in claims	8%	9%	8%	11%	12%	14%
Debtors out of insurance operations	32%	28%	30%	40%	52%	61%
Deferred acquisition costs	8%	7%	6%	11%	12%	17%

displayed in Table 2.4. "Investments" are real estate and financial assets. The "reinsurers' share in claims" is an estimate of the amount of future losses borne by reinsurers. This estimate stems from an application of the reinsurance treaties to the estimate of gross outstanding claims. "Debtors out of insurance operations" are, typically, policyholders or brokers owing premiums to the insurance company. "Deferred acquisition costs" correspond to the fact that insurance companies are allowed to spread the up-front acquisition cost of a new policy over the life of the policy. All these assets are expressed as percentages of the total amount of technical provisions (estimates of gross outstanding claims) at the end of the year.

Only investments and, to a lesser extent, claims on reinsurers are relatively easy to liquidate when cash is needed in order to settle claims. Premiums retained by the broker are generally only partially recovered, and at a very high cost, if the company is to be liquidated. Deferred acquisition costs are of course worthless when the firm stops being a going concern.

On the whole, these figures should have worried supervisors. The "good" assets, particularly investments, represented a sharply decreasing proportion of insurance claims over the period. Premiums were more and more difficult to collect. It might have been because Independent became disorganized and inefficient, or it might have been because the company started dealing with brokers it was less and less familiar with (and therefore it was less familiar with the risks accepted from these brokers), or even because some brokers started doubting Independent's creditworthiness. In any case, the solvency of Independent, measured as its ability to honor insurance claims in case of liquidation, very clearly deteriorated over the period.

The analysis of these very simple ratios is consistent with the following interpretation. Discovering that it was stuck with underpriced risks, the company decided to "gamble for resurrection." Namely, it started to estimate its future claims in an aggressive fashion to save time and try to develop new business in order to dilute future losses into a substantial turnover. This did not work. Instead, it led to a far more costly bankruptcy than if the firm had been restructured in an orderly fashion in 1996–97.

The information used in this analysis is of course very rough compared with that available to auditors, actuaries, and the regulator, who probably had much stronger signals about the company's distress over the period. Still, not much seems to have been done until the collapse. How the blame should be shared between the monitors, shareholders, and top management of Independent is beyond the scope of this book. But this case illustrates that the institutional design of prudential supervision is a crucial question, probably more important than the technical definition of prudential ratios. One plausible reason why the supervisory system turned out to be virtually pointless in Independent's case is that none of the agents who were endowed with the relevant information and control rights had the right incentives to undertake prompt corrective action when it was required.

2.2 Groupe des Assurances Nationales

Until the mid 1990s, most of the big players of the French financial-services industry were state-owned or recently privatized firms. They were run by a small and close-knit group of top-ranking civil servants (the so-called "Inspecteurs des Finances") who did not have much financial expertise or significant experience in running a for-profit organization and who were not subject to strong shareholder pressure. The best-known failure of this system was the large bankruptcy of Crédit Lyonnais.[3] This banking failure had an insurance equivalent, albeit on a smaller scale: Groupe des Assurances Nationales (GAN).

It might seem surprising that GAN, a well-established firm with a large market share in a fairly protected market, ended up losing a lot of money. We essentially view this as a consequence of perverse incentives for all players of the corporate game—shareholder, manager, regulator—due to inherent conflicts of interest.

First, the dominant shareholder, the French state, was a sleeping partner in the state-owned insurance sector. In practice, it was represented by the Minister of the Economy, Finance and Industry, supported by civil servants from the Treasury. The minister never provided firms with a clear strategic road map or profitability targets for the medium or long term, because it exceeded his political horizon. Politicians used state-owned insurance companies mostly as large reserves of cash that could be used to bail out or recapitalize distressed or undercapitalized firms in the public sector. They have never been deeply involved in defining or implementing strategies for their core insurance business. The administration in charge of monitoring government participation, the Treasury, did not really have any more incentive than politicians

---

[3] Crédit Lyonnais was bailed out by the French government in the early 1990s at a cost exceeding \$25 billion.

to maximize long-term shareholder value. Obtaining a position in this administration was the recommended first step on the road to obtaining a top management job in a bank or an insurance company. As a result, many of the civil servants in charge of monitoring state-owned financial institutions were dealing with a management comprised of their most successful and influential predecessors, often personally connected with members of the government. Tough monitoring under such circumstances could not really be expected.

Second, the top management was accordingly not subject to any kind of shareholder pressure, but had a very short horizon since it was almost systematically ousted and replaced each time a new Minister of the Economy, Finance and Industry was appointed, which occurred roughly every other year over the period. In the case of GAN, three different chairmen[4] had been in charge during the eight-year period we are studying. This mix of shareholder passivity and short-term horizon and lack of performance-based hiring decisions distorted the incentives of top management toward the fast buildup of large unprofitable empires, rather than the devotion of attention to risk-management issues.

Finally, the regulator, as a public authority, had a natural tendency to be lenient with state-owned firms, of course, because he viewed them as too big and too politically sensitive to fail, and because the prudential authorities were chaired by former civil servants belonging to the same elite as managers. For example, the head of the French Treasury, who was supposed to be a director of the state-owned insurance companies, also had a seat on the board of the French Insurance Supervisory Authority. Thus, the same person was in charge of representing the shareholders as a director as well as the policyholders as a regulator. This organization is of course at odds with the

---

[4]They were simultaneously chief executive officers, as is common in France.

modern views on efficient corporate governance that we will present in the rest of the book.

Unsurprisingly, most state-owned insurance companies did poorly in this environment—GAN being the one that experienced the most spectacular financial distress.

GAN was initially an insurance group, but eventually became a financial conglomerate, owning both banking and insurance subsidiaries after having taken over a state-owned banking group, CIC, in 1989. The main driver of this merger was the fact that the government was unwilling to capitalize state-owned banks with taxpayers' money, so that these banks meet the newly enforced Cooke ratio. In order to capitalize banks without injecting fresh money into the state-owned financial sector, the administration built hybrid groups such as GAN to make extensive use of double gearing. The group had four broad divisions: life and non-life insurance in France, international insurance, and banking. Three of them simultaneously experienced significant losses during the 1990s, with only life insurance being spared. Let us briefly describe what happened in the three distressed divisions.

Banking

CIC had two subsidiaries (UIC and SOFAL) that specialized in real estate (more precisely in loans to property developers). A real-estate bubble developed in France in the late 1980s and early 1990s. UIC–SOFAL was at the forefront of this speculative frenzy, its outstanding loans growing from Fr 27 billion in 1989 to Fr 50 billion in 1993. Very interestingly, the Cour des Comptes ("Court of Auditors"), a body with jurisdiction over financial matters for the public sector, had reported that state-owned institutions had a much higher exposure to this bubble than the private financial sector (Cour des Comptes 2000). As the bubble burst, the state-owned institutions had ratios of nonperforming loans over equity ranging from 20% to 119% (for UIC), while these ratios were below 10% in the private sector.

Subsequent audits revealed that the particularly strong exposure of UIC–SOFAL was due to poor internal organization and the absence of serious risk management within the banking group. The losses were estimated by the Cour des Comptes at Fr 30 billion at the end of 1996. These losses, even though they occurred in 1993, were concealed by UIC and GAN, who set up a defeasance scheme, which is, roughly speaking, a legal structure that allows a company to book losses on assets only as they materialize. As a result, GAN had apparently lost "only" 40% of its equity at the end of 1995 (Fr 13 billion), due to real-estate losses. Note that this attempt to conceal losses is reminiscent of Independent's behavior. Concealing losses was easier in the case of GAN because a conglomerate is by nature more opaque than a focused company.

International Activities

Strong evidence for the "empire-building" tendencies of state-owned insurers is that they all developed their international business quickly, by acquiring subsidiaries throughout the world, and lost a significant amount of money abroad during the subsequent years, until they decided to reduce their international exposure. GAN was no exception. The international turnover grew by 84% in 1990 from Fr 4.4 billion to Fr 8.7 billion. Cumulated losses over 1990 and 1991 were Fr 750 million and international operations only became (slightly) profitable again in 1993.

Domestic Non-Life Insurance

Finally, GAN developed a very aggressive new motor-insurance tariff, called "Tarif Bleu." Traditional insurance companies like GAN were losing market share to mutual companies like MACIF or MAAF, who had much lower acquisition and administration costs. This new tariff, meant to be competitive with respect to the quotes of mutuals, turned out to be ínsufficient. The profit and loss accounts of domestic non-life insurance from 1989 to 1995 are summarized in table 2.5.

Given the size of the portfolio, annual growth rates of 17%, 8%, and 15% from 1991 to 1993 were huge, well above market growth. The growth of losses was even more sizable, reflecting mispriced new business, and lagged, reflecting insufficient reserving.

GAN was eventually privatized in 1998 and acquired by the farmers' mutual insurance company GROUPAMA—but only after its bad assets had been defeased and the losses borne by taxpayers.

Besides offering an illustration of the consequences of bad governance and perverse incentives, this case has another point to recommend it: it shows that the received wisdom which states that a conglomerate is safe because it does not put "all its eggs in one basket" has to be treated with great caution. The GAN case suggests that the correlation between the business lines of a financial conglomerate is to some extent endogenous. Three out of four of GAN's activities experienced difficulties driven by the same factor: essentially that the management acted as an empire builder without being discouraged to do so by claimholders.

2.3 Equitable Life

(For this section we have benefited from helpful discussions with David Blake and we have made intensive use of his reports (downloadable at www.pensions-institute.org/reports/index.html) to tackle this case. However, the views expressed herein are not necessarily his.)

Before outlining this case, let us remind ourselves of the following elementary definition. A fixed-rate, single-life annuity is an insurance contract whereby the insurer commits to transform a given capital into a series of fixed payments between a given date and the death of the beneficiary. The annuity rate is

Table 2.5. Profit and loss accounts of GAN for French non-life business (billions of Fr).

Year	1989	1990	1991	1992	1993	1994	1995
Written premiums	8.9	9.1	10.6	11.5	13.2	13.4	14.0
Growth rate		2%	17%	8%	15%	1%	5%
Claims paid	6.5	6.7	7.4	9.3	11.4	13.0	11.3
Growth rate		3%	11%	25%	23%	14%	−14%
Change in the provisions	0.4	0.9	1.3	2.1	0.6	0.3	0.8
Growth rate		125%	53%	59%	−72%	−48%	175%
Operations expenses	2.8	2.9	3.3	3.5	3.9	2.8	3.2
Profit and loss	0.7	0.8	0.5	−1.1	−1.1	−1.2	−0.4

the price of the contract. For instance, a £6,000 annuity rate for a 60-year-old male means that if a male beneficiary provides the insurance company with capital of £100,000 when he is 60, he will get £6,000 each year from the insurance company until he dies. Thus, the higher the annuity rate, the cheaper the contract from the policyholder's standpoint. Such an annuity contract involves several risk transfers. First, the policyholder transfers a mortality risk and an investment risk to the insurance company: the insurance company makes a profit (respectively, a loss) if the beneficiary dies earlier (respectively, later) than expected, and if the assets in which the initial capital is invested yield more (respectively, less) than expected. Second, the beneficiary bears a counterparty risk. The insurance company may indeed go bankrupt and suspend or reduce annuities before he dies.

The Equitable Life Assurance Society (ELAS), a British mutual, sold pension annuities with guaranteed annuity rates (GARs) between 1957 and 1988. Such contracts consist of two phases: a saving phase and a decumulation phase. During the saving phase, say between ages 25 and 65, the policyholder invests part of her salary in the contract, and ELAS builds capital. When the policyholder retires at 65, ELAS transforms the capital into annuities: this is the decumulation phase. Thus, by granting GARs, the company commits to a given annuity rate for the decumulation phase at the beginning of the saving phase, when the capital that will be accumulated by the policyholder is still unknown. The company typically commits to an annuity rate for the decumulation phase more than 25 years before this phase begins (65 − 25 = 40 years in our example). It is therefore a risky bet on the long-run evolution of mortality and financial markets. In more financial terms, it amounts to endowing policyholders with long-run put options on the underlying risks, namely mortality and interest rates. As the decumulation phase starts, policyholders have the option to exercise their right to the initially guaranteed annuity rates. But they can also shop around for the current market rates in case mortality tables and discount rates yield annuity rates that are higher at the start of the decumulation phase than at the beginning of the contract. Thus, such options are valuable from the policyholders' standpoint because they have only a potential upside, no downside. Initially, such options were way "out-of-the-money." In other words, Equitable decided to lock in mortality tables and discount rates that yielded very low annuity rates compared with current market rates at the time. Thus, the options initially had no intrinsic value. This does not mean that they were worthless, however. In financial jargon, they had "time value," because interest rates and mortality could possibly decrease before the options matured, namely before policyholders retired. They actually did in 1994. However, from 1957 to 1994, ELAS neither priced the options—they were granted for free to policyholders who were willing to subscribe to them—nor hedged them.

It should be mentioned that many other British life-insurance companies granted such GARs throughout the 1960s and 1970s. Some plausible explanations for why they did so are

- that financial engineering and risk management were at the time burgeoning academic fields, hardly applied within the sector;
- that most insurers probably did not expect significant shifts in interest rates and mortality within the next thirty years;
- that some might have taken the view that whatever might happen was beyond their career horizon anyway.

In any case, they viewed GARs as pure marketing tools without important financial or technical implications.

We do not claim that granting GARs in the 1970s was an unreasonable decision at the time. It would be quite presumptuous to judge a decision that was made in a very specific macroeconomic context thirty years after the decision was made. We only argue that the way ELAS dealt with this risk once it materialized in the late 1980s was unsatisfactory, not that it was unreasonable to take this risk in the first place. ELAS is actually one of the companies that dealt with this issue most poorly during the 1980s and 1990s.

In 1982, a legal change gave pensioners the chance to shop around for an annuity. They became entitled to switch from one company to another as the contract entered the decumulation phase. This was a contractual event that ELAS might have exploited to stop offering GARs, but it did not seize this opportunity. This might suggest that the top management was still not fully aware of the risks at the time. ELAS only stopped offering GARs in 1988. But interestingly, it did not take any significant action to deal with the outstanding GARs at the time. This is reminiscent of Independent's behavior in 1998, eliminating "bad" risks from its portfolio without simultaneously increasing its reserves for outstanding claims. Another analogy with Independent is that ELAS apparently tried to dilute the GARs issue into a quickly growing non-GAR business. Table 2.6 shows ELAS's premium income and total assets between 1990 and 2000.

As a result of this dilution, 75% of the value of the fund was owed to non-GAR policyholders by 2001. Over a longer time interval, because the production cycle is very stretched in life insurance, ELAS did very much the same as Independent. It expanded new business, while not dealing with the GAR issue in a timely fashion in order to cut losses. There were a number of ways to deal with it in the late 1980s/early 1990s, and they were implemented by some of ELAS's competitors. The most natural one is the insurance analogue of defeasance structures in banking. It amounts to ring-fencing GAR contracts in a separate fund, and capping the losses on the runoff by a reinsurance contract. The management of the runoff may be outsourced, and the reinsurance contract retroceded to institutions that have particular expertise in managing and hedging

Table 2.6. Premium income and total assets of Equitable.
(Source: Blake (2001).)

Year	Premium income (millions of pounds)	Total assets (millions of pounds)
1990	1,346	5,786
1991	1,715	7,368
1992	1,877	9,497
1993	2,101	13,407
1994	2,052	13,545
1995	2,362	16,612
1996	2,830	19,305
1997	3,452	23,676
1998	3,730	28,068
1999	3,484	32,902
2000	2,941	34,754

such risks. In this case, a sizable cost is paid up front, but once and for all. One of the reasons the top management of ELAS had no incentive to cut losses in this way might have been because ELAS is a mutual company. By definition, there was no sophisticated long-term investor around, with the incentive to protect her stake and deal with GARs before it became too painful. Interestingly, some of ELAS's competitors, which had been demutualized during the 1980s and 1990s and acquired by other financial institutions, have implemented this type of solution.

Instead, ELAS only tackled this issue in 1994, after the GAR options became in the money at the end of 1993 and its liabilities became obviously underestimated, even without taking into account the time value of put options. But dealing with this issue was difficult at the time. Being a mutual, ELAS had, by definition, no investors to tap (other than its customers) in order to finance the losses materializing from naked put options. It did so by introducing a differential final bonus policy. Non-GAR policyholders were endowed with a higher final bonus than those with GARs. In a sense, as pointed out by Blake (2001, p. 5), this measure made explicit the fact that non-GAR policyholders were (unwitting) sellers of options to GAR policyholders. If the difference in bonuses equals the value of the options that GAR policyholders have subscribed to, then it "fairly" compensates non-GAR policyholders for granting them such options. ELAS considered such a measure to be in compliance with its bylaws. Of course, a number of GAR policyholders were unsatisfied with this, arguing that it made GARs worthless. ELAS initiated an action in the High Court in London to resolve the issue. The case ended up in the House of Lords.

In July 2000, the House of Lords ruled that all policyholders should receive equal treatment, and that the portfolio of GAR policies could not be ring-fenced and managed separately from the non-GAR ones. This decision raises two issues.

First, it must be emphasized that during the six years that elapsed between the introduction of ELAS's differential bonus policy and this ruling, many new non-GAR premiums were paid. While ELAS had identified the risks associated with GARs (it stopped offering them in 1988), it failed to acknowledge the magnitude of this risk in its financial statements through the recording of a reserve equal to the value of the options. This made ELAS look artificially rich over the period, and enabled it to try to dilute the GAR losses in a very rapidly growing new business. As in the Independent case, this behavior is consistent with a "gamble for resurrection."

Second, as pointed out by Blake (2001, p. 4), the Lords' decision was internally inconsistent. On the one hand, it stated that all policyholders invested in the same pool of assets should be treated equally. But GAR and non-GAR policyholders had claims of different seniorities on the same pool of assets. It was thus impossible to treat them equally. On the other hand, it also ruled out the possibility of ring-fencing GAR contracts and dedicating assets to them. As a result of this decision, ELAS was left without a clear road map to solve the GARs problem.

On the whole, the unsatisfactory timing and content of this decision shows the importance of having such issues dealt with in a timely fashion by a specialized authority endowed with more financial expertise and faster procedures than the general legal system.

The total cost of the decision for ELAS was estimated to be £1.5 billion (£200 million to correct the low bonuses between 1994 and 2000, and the remainder to cover future shortfalls). This represented about 25% of GAR policy values. In February 2001, ELAS transferred a £500 million portfolio of not-for-profit business to Halifax plc. Halifax committed to invest an additional £500 million if, broadly speaking, a compromise was found to solve the GAR problem by 2002. On July 16, 2001, partly due to falling stock markets, all policy values were reduced by 16%. Halifax's conditional commitment to invest an additional £500 million was of course crucial to ELAS, who proposed the following compromise scheme proposal (CSP) to solve the GAR problem. The CSP consisted in

- uplifting GAR policy values by 17.5% in exchange for GAR policyholders giving up their right to a guaranteed annuity rate; and

- uplifting non-GAR policies values by 2.5% in exchange for a commitment to renounce claims for misselling.

The CSP had to be approved by a majority of voting policyholders (and by 75% by policy values). A quasi-unanimity of policyholders voted in favor of the CSP on January 28, 2002. This was probably as a result of policyholders having no choice but to accept the CSP to get Halifax's money, more than as a result of genuine enthusiasm.

Unfortunately, this was not the end of ELAS's troubles. While it had stopped offering GAR pension annuities in 1988, it continued, until 1996, granting other free put options, such as guaranteed interest rates (GIRs), during the savings phase of the contracts. The guaranteed rate was 3.5%, and applied to roughly 75% of the portfolio, an ambitious target in the distressed financial markets of 2001. As a result, the for-profit fund was still in a difficult situation after the CSP had been approved, facing exactly the same problem of a very inconsistent structure that pooled the assets for different classes of liabilities. On the whole, losses were still not cut 15 years after the GAR problem was unambiguously identified by ELAS's top management.

2.4 Europavie

Europavie was the first life-insurance company to go bankrupt in France since World War II.[5] It was a small company, with insurance liabilities of about Fr 350 million in a market of Fr 500 billion. Still, the shock was sufficiently important to trigger a significant reaction: the creation of a life-insurance guarantee fund.

Europavie was created in 1987 by a group of brokers. In general, brokers set up insurance companies when they are not satisfied with the contracts available in the market, and want to supply their own contracts more suited to their customers' needs. Europavie specialized in unit-linked contracts backed by real estate. A unit-linked life-insurance contract is a contract that does not guarantee fixed cash payments, but instead a fixed number of shares in some investment vehicle, typically a mutual fund. Europavie issued such contracts backed by real-estate funds. Such contracts are typically safe from a prudential

---

[5] It is fair to say that, until the mid 1980s, the safety of the French life-insurance market owed much to lack of competition and to unfairly loaded contracts.

standpoint since the investment risk is borne by policyholders, not by the company. By construction, assets match liabilities. However, Europavie guaranteed a high interest rate, 8%, on premiums invested in these contracts. This very unreasonable promise got the company into trouble in the early 1990s, as the French real-estate bubble burst. A diversified conglomerate, Thinet, took it over in 1994. Thinet had not specialized in the financial-services industry up to that point, but in various nonfinancial activities and in real estate. Acquiring this company was a cheap way to finance real-estate operations. We note in passing that this takeover was authorized by the French regulator, while the association of French insurers denied membership to the company in 1987 and 1994. Thinet continued to develop unit-linked contracts backed by real estate and had doubled the turnover by 1996. From 1996 onwards, instead of realizing losses in real estate, Europavie used some of its general assets to redeem contracts. In 1997, BVH, a German bank subsidiary of Thinet, in which a significant part of Europavie's general assets were deposited, became insolvent. The German banking regulator took disciplinary action. As a result, the whole group went bust and organized its insolvency. Because of the default of BVH and the earlier realization of liquid assets to redeem contracts, Europavie ended up with insufficient, poorly performing, and illiquid assets to back its liabilities. The eventual shortage was Fr 120 million, more than one-third of its insurance liabilities.

We do not dwell on the technical details of this case because this broad picture is sufficiently enlightening. Obviously, this company had been run by a top management and inside shareholders without any kind of insurance expertise—behavior that was at least irresponsible, if not fraudulent. The main lesson we draw from this case is that, from a prudential point of view, conglomerates merit particular attention. Thinet was a small conglomerate. But size is not the primary concern when it comes to conglomerates. The point is that Thinet was involved in various activities in various European countries. Because regulators, e.g., the French insurance supervisor and German banking regulator, did not cooperate fully, the conglomerate was very opaque to them. In the absence of consolidated supervision, assessing the actual situation of each division or subsidiary of a conglomerate is difficult. Moreover, once the group is in distress, shareholders have a strong advantage over uncoordinated regulators and can organize the insolvency of the company in their own interests: namely, minimize the recovery value of policyholders' claims by exploiting legal loopholes and discrepancies between local bankruptcy laws.[6]

2.5 Why Are Insurers Subject to Prudential Regulation? A First Pass

Although these four firms were operating in different lines of business within different countries, it is interesting to note that their episodes of distress have several features in common. The basic scenario is the same: after an initial unexpected shock on assets (e.g., the bursting of the real-estate bubble for GAN and Europavie) or liabilities (e.g., GAR entering the money for Equitable), the net wealth of the company decreases. But only company insiders, namely the top management and possibly some inside shareholders, seem to react to this in the first place. Instead of cutting their losses, they find it optimal to "gamble for resurrection," and they are correct from their standpoint. If this does not work, as was the case in the examples presented above, policyholders end up much poorer than before the insiders gambled for resurrection. Why is this scheme more likely to occur and to be more costly for insurance companies than for nonfinancial firms or banks? We believe that such

---

[6] This specificity is one of the reasons why we outline specific recommendations for the supervision of financial conglomerates in chapter 8.

corporate governance issues are due to a combination of two factors.

First, the *inversion of the production cycle* makes it easy for the top management of insurance companies to conceal difficulties while taking risky bets. If these bets fail, further future losses have to be compensated by taking even riskier bets. Thus, that losses do not materialize immediately into liquidity needs creates room for an endogenous amplification of exogenous shocks because of excessive risk taking. Second, the *absence of a tough, sophisticated claimholder* willing to cut his/her losses makes it unlikely that this spiral will end before a liquidity problem reveals the actual magnitude of the insolvency problem.

We believe that coping with these two factors is the raison d'être of prudential regulation. We elaborate on this main point in chapters 4 and 5. Before that, chapter 3 describes the main features of prudential systems, and summarizes the risk-theoretic analysis of prudential regulation.

3

The State of the Art in Prudential Regulation

In this chapter, we aim to offer a broad picture of the current dominant views on the prudential regulation of insurance companies. We start by explaining the main features of the prudential system. We go on to describe the main theoretical framework that practitioners have in mind when debating prudential regulation, and finally we emphasize what we consider to be the shortcomings of this theoretical framework.

3.1 The Main Features of Prudential Systems

Prudential systems basically have two components.

(i) Prudential regulations stating that insurance companies

(a) must estimate their outstanding liabilities toward policyholders in a sufficiently conservative fashion;

(b) must invest in assets whose aggregate liquidity and risk profile is appropriate with respect to those liabilities;

(c) must finance an excess of such assets over such estimates with their own capital.

(ii) Supervisory authorities in charge of

(a) monitoring that insurance companies comply with prudential regulations;

(b) adopting corrective measures for the insurers that do not comply with these rules;

(c) managing, in some countries, the guarantee funds that have been created to insure policyholders against the failure of their insurer.

This definition is sufficiently broad to encompass most prudential systems. The institutional details differ significantly across countries, however. Let us, for example, compare the ways in which insurers' balance sheets are constrained on each side of the Atlantic: in U.S. and European markets.

In Europe, solvency requirements build on two rules. First, the estimates of insurance liabilities (referred to as "technical provisions" in European law) must be covered by an equal amount of qualified assets. To qualify, assets must be sufficiently diversified, i.e., spread across categories (stocks, fixed income, real estate, etc.) and counterparties, the limits for each line being expressed as a percentage of the technical provisions. This percentage is larger when the asset is safe (e.g., government bonds) or liquid (e.g., stocks listed on a major exchange). Second, insurance companies must meet the European solvency margin. Roughly speaking, this states that the book value of a firm's equity must exceed some threshold, expressed as a piecewise-linear function of premiums (non-life insurance) or reserves (life insurance) multiplied by reinsurance cession rates.

In the United States, the solvency requirement is the so-called risk-based capital (RBC). The minimal capital requirement is a complex (nonlinear) function of several variables used as proxies for the several risks facing an insurance company: premiums and their evolution, reserves and their runoff in each business line, exposure by counterparty and asset class, off-balance-sheet operations. This requirement has to be met under accounting standards (statutory accounting principles, or SAPs) that are more conservative than the ones used for the public report (Generally Accepted Accounting Principles, or GAAPs). Even though they lead to quantitatively different outcomes, the European and U.S. solvency requirements both consist in imposing a lower bound on the net equity of insurance companies, estimated in a particularly conservative fashion.

In these examples, and more generally, prudential rules are of course very sensitive to the way items are evaluated on both sides of insurers' balance sheets: the primitives of prudential standards are accounting and actuarial standards. How to set such standards is a difficult and controversial topic in practice. This is illustrated by the recent fierce opposition of the financial institutions and regulators of some European countries to the proposals of the International Accounting Standards Committee toward international accounting rules based on so-called "fair valuation." The U.S. choice of a specific supervisory accounting standard, distinct from the general one, has both drawbacks and advantages, discussed later in this book.

Not only prudential rules but also the design and organization of supervisory authorities are very diverse across countries. For instance, in the United Kingdom, the ongoing monitoring of the reserving policy is performed by appointed actuaries hired by insurance companies in a competitive market, very much like auditing firms. In France, this task is performed by a public monopoly, employing civil servants with indefinite tenure. Another important distinction across countries is whether the insurance regulator is a division of an authority in charge of other financial institutions (as it is in the United Kingdom, Japan, Germany, Australia, Singapore, and other countries) or whether it is an autonomous entity (as it is in the United States, France, Italy, and Spain).

This diversity of rules and institutions shows that there is no widespread consensus on the optimal organization of prudential systems, thereby suggesting that there may be disagreement on the *purpose* of these systems as well.

The evolution of insurance activities over the last twenty years—the emergence of global groups such as AIG or AXA, the increased complexity of risk-management techniques and investment strategies, increased competition—is certainly good news for the efficiency of the industry. But it implies that prompt corrective action of prudential authorities becomes more crucial than ever as an insurance company becomes financially distressed.

Several countries acknowledged this evolution, and therefore undertook in-depth reform of their supervisory systems during the 1990s. In the United States, for instance, the National Association of Insurance Commissioners (NAIC) has organized a sophisticated system, Financial Analysis and Surveillance Tracking (FAST), aimed at early detection of companies experiencing financial distress. This system is based on detailed information about companies' balance sheets and income statements, collected in the Insurance Regulatory Information System (IRIS) and summarized by several accounting ratios (12 for life/health insurers, 11 for property/casualty insurers). These complex regulatory/supervisory systems have been in place since 1993–94, following an impressive wave of insurance failures.

Important reforms of regulatory/supervisory systems are also going on in many countries. For example, Australia has enacted a "General Insurance Reform Act" (effective from July 2002), which sets new prudential standards for general insurance companies. The Australian Prudential Regulation Authority (APRA) has defined six prudential standards, covering liability valuation, capital adequacy, reinsurance, risk management, transfer and amalgamation of insurance business, and national investments. Similarly, in the United Kingdom, the Financial Services Authority (FSA), which regulates the whole financial-services industry (including banks and insurance companies) has issued an "Integrated Prudential Sourcebook." This sourcebook aims to integrate prudential principles across the whole field of financial services. The idea is to organize prudential standards by risk factor (market, credit, operational, insurance, and group risk), not according to whether the firm is a bank, an insurance company, or an investment firm. The new sourcebook also requires systematic use of internal systems of stress testing by insurance companies, so as to determine by themselves the level of resources they need to meet the risks inherent to their business. Finally, the European Commission has issued one new directive (known as "Solvency I") and a proposal for a second (known as "Solvency II"). Solvency I, introduced in October 2000, covers proposals on solvency margin requirements for both life and non-life insurers. It amends the European Commission's Action Plan for a single internal market in financial services, which was adopted in May 1999. Solvency II is a proposed directive on prudential supervision of financial conglomerates. It covers issues such as double gearing (i.e., having the same capital counted twice, and so being used simultaneously as a buffer against risk in two different entities of the same financial conglomerate), and the removal of inconsistencies between different types of regulation for banking and insurance activities.

In addition to these ongoing reforms, several international bodies are working on changes to the prudential regulation of insurance. The International Association of Insurance Supervisors (IAIS) has published a paper on solvency requirements, aimed at harmonizing solvency principles among its country members. The International Actuarial Association (IAA) has also sent a written response to the reform of the Basel Committee prudential standards for banks (this reform is known as Basel II). The IAA suggests that there is a need for "consistent accounting for prudential supervision regimes that operate across banking, insurance and investment management." Finally, as already mentioned, the International Accounting Standards Body (IASB) is seeking to develop an international standard on accounting for insurance contracts.

We will argue in this book that, despite these developments, several spectacular insurance failures could have been very significantly mitigated if supervisors had intervened earlier, and that such early interventions would have been feasible under more efficient supervisory mechanisms. The economic analysis of insurance regulation we develop suggests that there is room for supervisory systems dealing more satisfactorily with distressed firms, while being less costly to the well-functioning ones. But let us first describe the standard actuarial approach to prudential regulation.

3.2   Regulation and Ruin Theory: Controlling the Probability of Failure

The standard theoretical approach underlying insurance regulation originates in actuarial methods, and more specifically in ruin theory. It is important to outline this theory, and then to discuss its limits, because it is the one that most insurance practitioners or regulators have in mind when thinking about insurance regulation, partly of course because a number of them have been trained as actuaries.

Broadly speaking, this approach posits that the aim of prudential regulation is to ensure that the probability of ruin of insurance companies is below some given "acceptable" value. The second assumption is that the main tool available to the regulator to reach this aim is to set a mandatory solvency margin, namely the minimum amount of a firm's own equity that may be used as a buffer. While this approach is traditional and classic in the insurance industry, it is interesting to note that a similar view recently became influential in banking, with the rise of "Value-at-Risk" methods to manage market and credit risks. These methods may involve very-high-tech modeling tools, but they hinge on the same simple principles.

Let us illustrate this approach through the stylized example of an insurance company characterized by the following simplified balance sheet:

Assets A Reserves R
Equity E

At this stage, we neglect asset risk, and thus assume that the assets of this company are comprised of riskless investments, with a rate of return that we normalize to zero. We assume that the company does not underwrite new risks. The profits and losses of the company are determined by the runoff, or the difference between the current estimates of future claims, namely the reserves R, and their eventual costs.

Defining $(1 + \tilde{x})$ as the random variable that characterizes the ratio final cost/reserves, failure occurs at the end of the reference period when final cost $R(1 + \tilde{x})$ exceeds the value of assets:

$$R(1 + \tilde{x}) > A = R + E.$$

Subtracting R from both sides and then dividing by R, we see that failure is characterized by the stochastic event

$$\tilde{x} > E/R.$$

Therefore, if the probability distribution of the ratio $\tilde{x}$, Φ, has been estimated by statistical methods, the probability of failure can be estimated as

$$\Pr(\tilde{x} > E/R) = 1 - \Phi(E/R).$$

If m represents the 99% quantile of the probability distribution of $\tilde{x}$ (see figure 3.1), we see that imposing a minimum margin requirement limits the probability of failure below 1%:

$$\frac{\text{Equity}}{\text{Premiums}} \geqslant m \iff \Pr(\text{Failure}) \leqslant 1 - \Phi(m) = 1.$$

Ruin theory essentially aims to solve more-sophisticated, dynamic versions of this model in order to estimate the minimum solvency margin needed to obtain a survival probability of at least 99% (for example) over a given, possibly long, time horizon.

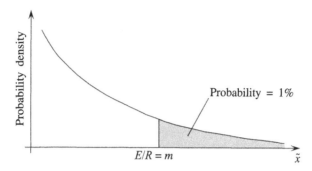

Figure 3.1.   Margin requirement for a probability of ruin of 1%.

Let us now account for the riskiness of assets as follows. Consider a situation where the insurer has invested in two types of asset: riskless assets, with a rate of return normalized to zero; and risky assets, with a random rate of return $\tilde{r}$. The balance sheet becomes

Riskless assets A_0	Reserves R
Risky assets A_1	Equity E

In this case, failure occurs when

$$A_0 + A_1(1 + \tilde{r}) < R(1 + \tilde{x}).$$

Since $A_0 + A_1 = R + E$, this is equivalent to

$$\tilde{y} < -E,$$

where $\tilde{y} = A_1\tilde{r} - R\tilde{x}$ denotes the net operating profit (the difference between financial income and runoff). Assuming that $\tilde{y}$ can be approximated by a normal distribution with mean 0 and variance σ_y^2, the probability of failure is approximated by $N(-E/\sigma_y)$, where N is the distribution of a standard normal variable. Since the 1% lower quantile of this distribution is approximately -2, the probability of failure will be less than 1% if E is at least equal to $2\sigma_y$. Now σ_y can be computed easily:

$$\sigma_y = \sqrt{A_1^2\sigma_r^2 + R^2\sigma_x^2},$$

where σ_r^2 denotes the variance of risky assets' returns and σ_x^2 denotes the variance of the loss ratio, and assuming that these two risks are independent. Therefore, the way to limit the probability of failure to a predetermined threshold is to impose a minimum capital requirement whose computation is reminiscent of the U.S. RBC:

$$\text{Equity} \geqslant \sqrt{4A_1^2\sigma_r^2 + 4R^2\sigma_x^2}.$$

The assumption underlying such ratios, that technical and financial risks are independent, seems to be a heroic one. Casual evidence suggests that distressed insurance companies tend to experience financial and operational difficulties simultaneously (remember the GAN case). Thus, assuming that these risks are positively correlated seems more realistic. This correlation is of course related to the fact that both risks are driven by common factors, namely the organizational inefficiency of the company and the poor quality of its governance.

Practical Limits of Ruin Theory

Even if the actuarial approach provides theoretical foundations for margin requirements and RBC-type formulas, these formulas do not seem particularly good at predicting failures or financial distress in practice. Several scholars (Cummins et al. 1995, 1999; Grace et al. 1993) have studied the predictive power of the RBC and FAST scores for forecasting the failure or financial distress of U.S. insurance companies. All of these studies have concluded that the predictive power of these techniques is very weak.[1] Other methods, based on cash-flow simulations, seem to work better. In any case, it is fair to say that no simple method is available for predicting the financial

---

[1] Note that this does not necessarily imply that these scores are "wrong." It may simply be that statistical models of insurance failures are bound to be rejected because the sample of failed insurance companies is too small.

distress of insurance companies. It seems unrealistic to assume that supervisory agencies can implement a universal formula for limiting the probability of failures of insurance companies to an exogenous maximum.

Conceptual Limits of Ruin Theory

Ruin theory does not explain why regulating the probability of ruin is desirable. Most corporate-finance textbooks start out with the well-known irrelevance result of Modigliani and Miller (1958). This result states that, without any friction on capital markets, the debt to equity ratio of a firm should have no impact on its total value. Indeed, the capital structure only impacts on the way the total value of the firm is split between shareholders and debtholders.

If we apply the Modigliani–Miller theorem to insurance companies, it is not obvious why capping the probability of ruin should create any value. Asking the shareholders of an insurance company to pledge assets to cover the insurance liabilities in excess of collected premiums should be neutral in a frictionless world. Policyholders should, indeed, be willing to pay higher insurance premiums because this pledge reduces the insurer's probability of default. But this benefit would be exactly offset by the cost of newly committed capital, at least if there is no arbitrage opportunity.

The assumption of perfect, frictionless capital markets that underlies this Modigliani–Miller irrelevance result is not satisfied in practice. Corporate-finance theory has put forward several reasons why capital structure matters. We will explore some of them and apply them to insurance throughout the rest of the book. But ruin theory is in general developed in stylized, ideal models where none of the imperfections which may justify the relevance of capital structure are present. In other words, ruin theory studies prudential regulation in models where prudential regulation is pointless!

Ruin theory does not tell us why capital requirements are the best way to cap the probability of ruin. Even if one takes for granted that the probability of failure of insurance companies has to be regulated, it is still not clear why the best control for this probability is the capital of insurance companies. To motivate this point, let us slightly enrich the elementary model of ruin theory used in this chapter by modeling the insurance portfolio more explicitly.

Consider an insurer with equity E and a portfolio of N independent and identically distributed risks. Denote by $\tilde{S}_i$ the random variable representing the loss derived from risk i, during the relevant time period, and for $i = 1, \ldots, N$. We assume that each $\tilde{S}_i$ has a mean μ (normalized to 1) and a standard deviation σ. Each risk is covered by a premium $1 + \rho$, where $\rho > 0$ represents the loading factor (net of reinsurance premiums).

The probability of ruin P_r is thus

$$\Pr(E + N(1 + \rho) < \tilde{S}_1 + \tilde{S}_2 + \cdots + \tilde{S}_N)$$
$$= \Pr(\tilde{S}_1 + \tilde{S}_2 + \cdots + \tilde{S}_N - N > E + N\rho).$$

By virtue of Chebyshev's inequality,[2] one has

$$P_r \leqslant \frac{N\sigma^2}{(E + N\rho)^2} = \frac{1}{\beta^2}, \quad \text{where } \beta = \frac{E + N\rho}{\sqrt{N}\sigma}.$$

Chebyshev's inequality yields a very conservative upper bound for the probability of ruin, only used here for illustrative purposes. In ruin theory, β is usually referred to as the security coefficient. Increasing β amounts to reducing the probability of ruin. This expression shows that there are many ways to raise β. Increasing E by means of capital requirements

---

[2] Chebyshev's inequality states that the probability that a zero-mean random variable $\tilde{Y}$ exceeds some threshold α is less than $\mathrm{var}(\tilde{Y})/\alpha^2$. Here we take $\tilde{Y} = \tilde{S}_1 + \cdots + \tilde{S}_N - N$ and $\alpha = E + N\rho$. Since individual losses are independent, the variance of $\tilde{Y}$ equals $N\sigma^2$.

is, of course, one of them, but there are other methods, like increasing N or ρ, or reducing σ.

Thus, instead of imposing capital requirements, why not require insurance companies to load their premiums sufficiently, buy a sufficient amount of reinsurance to reduce σ, or even hold sufficiently large portfolios?

Any sensible practitioner or economist has an obvious answer to this. Modification of the underwriting policy, either by raising the tariffs or the size of the portfolio, has to be carried out very cautiously. Otherwise, for reasons of informational asymmetry in particular, the complex adverse effects of such strategies on the nature of underwritten risks may well overcome the benefits. Remember that some of the cases of distressed companies described in chapter 2 suggest that a sudden change in underwriting practices often increases the risk of failure.

Similarly, reinsurance reduces the volatility of losses σ, but also the expected profit ratio (net loading factor) ρ, because some fraction of the premiums are used to reward reinsurers' risk taking. Whether these two effects result in an increase or a decrease of the probability of ruin depends on the design and pricing of the reinsurance treaty.

On the whole, it is hard to believe that regulators would be able to use such alternative tools to control for the probability of ruin and to account properly for their adverse effects. The information-collection and technical skills required to achieve this are too important. But are things really different for capital requirements?

Ruin theory neglects the market's response to regulation.   Let us again assume that it is desirable to limit the occurrence of ruin due to bad luck. Let us further assume that the only tool available to the regulator to achieve this aim is a capital requirement. Ruin theory still misses the point that such a tool has to be handled very carefully in order to deliver an appropriate outcome. This approach views insurance companies as "black boxes" transforming premiums into random variables. But insurance companies are firms that respond optimally to their economic environment and business conditions. Imposing a capital requirement impacts on the cost of one of the crucial inputs of the insurance production function: capital. Therefore, any analysis of the impact of capital requirements should take into account the response of insurance companies to those new production costs.

The theoretical study of this response has been carried out in the banking sector by, among others, Kim and Santomero (1988) and Rochet (1992). These studies show that ill-designed capital requirements may lead to "regulatory arbitrage" by banks, namely activities aimed at reducing their regulatory capital requirement, while actually *increasing* their risk of failure. This explains why the Basel Committee has expended a lot of effort reforming the Cooke ratio toward a more risk-based approach. Regarding insurance, this suggests that the U.S. system of RBC, aimed at reflecting the riskiness of assets and insurance portfolios better than the European solvency margin, may deal better with regulatory arbitrage. However, it is not clear how a "one-size-fits-all" regulation, implemented by a regulator who cannot possibly know as much about firms as the firms themselves, could really be risk based, and hence not distort insurers' strategies toward inefficient portfolios.

3.3 Conclusions

Not How? But Why?

To sum up, ruin theory takes for granted that

(i) the probability of failure of insurance companies has to be regulated;

(ii) the best way to do so is to set a capital requirement.

Ruin theory then focuses on the practical calibration of capital requirements that ensure a sufficiently low probability of failure, given the distribution of the risks that affect the net wealth of insurance companies.

Our approach will dramatically differ from this one. We do not want to assume a particular design or aim for prudential regulation. Instead, we are primarily interested in identifying the fundamental economic reasons why insurance companies, unlike other firms, should be subject to some form of prudential regulation.

In the next two chapters, we describe what we view as the essential rationales for prudential regulation in the insurance industry: inversion of the production cycle and absence of a tough claimholder.

Regulating the Regulator

At this stage, it is important to stress that the imperfections of the insurance market that we identify are not sufficient to warrant a role for insurance regulation. In general, the existence of a market failure is necessary, but not sufficient, to warrant a role for regulation. *It must also be the case that the cost of regulation is smaller than its benefits.*

The most important costs of regulation stem from the fact that the regulatory entity may pursue objectives that are very different from those it is initially assigned. The only way to cope with this issue is to design regulation very carefully, in a way that ensures that the self-interests of the regulators are in line with the objectives of the regulation. We offer practical ways of achieving this aim and of providing the right incentives to the regulators in chapter 6 of the book.

4

Inversion of the Production Cycle and Capital Structure of Insurance Companies

4.1 Inversion of the Production Cycle in the Insurance Industry

As is particularly clear in the Independent case, the reason insurance companies are likely to suffer from important agency problems[1] is the well-known inversion of the production cycle in the insurance industry. Unlike most other goods and services, insurance services are only produced *after* they are purchased by policyholders. For example, in property/casualty insurance, premiums are typically paid by policyholders when the contract is signed, but compensation is paid by insurers only after a claim is made and settled, which may take several years. This is so because it would be difficult in practice to collect premiums *ex post* from all the policyholders who did not experience a significant loss. In life or professional liability insurance, the time interval between the payment of premiums and the payment of compensation (the "length of the production cycle") may exceed twenty years. Thus, the true production costs of an insurance company (claims) are

---

[1] In economists' jargon, "agency problems" refer to conflicts of interests within firms (e.g., conflicts between owners and managers, or between shareholders and creditors).

revealed only a long time after business has been underwritten and premiums cashed in. Moreover, the final losses depend heavily upon the insurers' ability and efforts to mitigate losses during the runoff period.[2] The skills of a company's claims managers and their diligence in loss mitigation are hard to verify by nonexpert outsiders. It is not very difficult, indeed, for a claims manager to underreserve (namely, underestimate insurance liabilities in the books of the company) over the course of several years. Thus, she can enter into a Ponzi scheme: financing losses on the runoff of past underwriting years by underreserving for the recent ones, thus concealing losses or management mistakes for quite a long time. In other words, illiquidity does not precede insolvency for insurance companies, whereas this is often the case in other industries. This phenomenon is an important concern in insurance, as epitomized by the following statement from Warren Buffet[3] in the Berkshire Hathaway Shareholders Letter of 2002:

> I can promise you that our top priority going forward is to avoid inadequate reserving. But I can't guarantee success. The natural tendency of most casualty-insurance managers is to underreserve, and they must have a particular mindset—which, it may surprise you, has nothing to do with actuarial expertise—if they are to overcome this devastating bias.

Because of the inversion of the production cycle, a negative shock (due to bad luck) on the net wealth of an insurance company may result years later in a very severe bankruptcy. But the bulk of the eventual loss is mainly a consequence of the corporate governance problem induced by the initial shock, not a direct consequence of the shock itself. In other words,

---

[2] The runoff period is the time interval between the occurrence of claims and their settlements, and exceeds two years for many business lines.

[3] Warren Buffet achieved one of the most impressive recent U.S. insurance successes with the build-up of Berkshire Hathaway.

severe distress for insurers generally results from two separate causes that reinforce each other: corporate governance problems and insufficient capitalization. Corporate governance problems refer to situations in which the top management of a firm consistently makes decisions that undermine the future of the firm. Such decisions can be bad or even fraudulent investments, inaccurate reinsurance or financial policy, excessive external growth, or inappropriate commercial policy (underwriting "bad" risks or underpricing contracts). They occur when stockholders and/or directors lose control of the top management. Insufficient capitalization may stem from a persistent deterioration of profitability and/or catastrophic losses due to adverse economic conditions. It results in changes in the risk preference of stockholders, who develop strategies of betting for survival and knowingly encourage management to adopt excessively risky policies. Betting for survival means choosing projects that result in a large profit with a small probability or in a loss with a large probability. It is optimal from the standpoint of stockholders of poorly capitalized firms since most of the losses are borne by debtholders in this case. These two causes lead to the same consequences and, of course, tend to reinforce each other: management tends to take excessive risks when profitability deteriorates, and these excessive risks are likely to later materialize in a further deterioration of profitability.

Modern corporate-finance theory has shown that the capital structure of firms is a tool with which to discipline the management and cope with such problems. We shall now describe these findings and discuss their application to capital requirements for insurance companies.

4.2 An Analogy between Insurance Capital and Deductibles in Insurance Contracts

As briefly mentioned in the previous chapter, the starting point of modern corporate-finance theory is the irrelevance result

due to Modigliani and Miller (1958): when financial markets are efficient, capital structure does not impact the total
value of firms. In perfect financial markets, capital structure
is just a way to slice the "corporate pie." But the way a pie
is sliced has no impact on its size! There is an easy way to
understand this result. If investors can borrow without constraints, and at the same cost as firms, and invest the proceeds
in the shares of an unlevered firm, they can build a portfolio
on their own which is equivalent to holding the stock of the
same firm with leverage. There is no capital structure decided
by the firm which cannot be replicated by investors. Hence,
capital structures decided by firms are irrelevant—investors
can do or undo them by choosing their own leverage. This
result is obviously very unrealistic! Anyone with some practical business experience would acknowledge that capital structure *does* matter in practice. But this is precisely why the
Modigliani–Miller theorem is a very interesting starting point
for corporate-finance theory. It pins down the assumptions that
need to be relaxed in order to obtain more realistic models
of financial markets: models in which capital structure matters. Relaxing these assumptions has been the main agenda
of corporate-finance theory over the last thirty years. In this
chapter, we describe some of the important findings of modern
corporate finance theory, and apply these findings to the analysis of the role of prudential capital requirements for insurance
companies.

To make this analysis of capital requirements more concrete, let us use a formal analogy (that we hope is illuminating) between the capital of insurance companies and the
deductibles of insurance contracts. To see why such an analogy makes sense, let us first compare the role of equity in
insurance companies and in industrial firms. For nonfinancial
firms, equity may be used to finance productive assets (like
plants) or as working capital during production cycles, namely
to finance the liquidity gap due to the fact that inputs have to

be bought before outputs are sold. Insurance capital is special: it meets none of these needs. The productive assets (headquarters, software, etc.) are a very marginal part of insurance total assets. The bulk of these assets is financial. And because of the inversion of the production cycle, insurance companies do not need working capital: they sell outputs before buying inputs. Therefore, insurance capital is merely a pure buffer. The shareholders of an insurance company bear the first losses of the company up to the amount of capital they have thrown in. Only when these losses exceed the value of equity do policyholders bear the excess part. Thus, for an insurance company that does not need to finance its production cycle, equity is very much like a deductible in an insurance contract, which leaves the first losses of each event to the purchaser of insurance. The correspondence is as follows:

Insurance contract	$\Longleftrightarrow$	Capital structure
Policyholder	$\Longleftrightarrow$	Shareholder
Insurance company	$\Longleftrightarrow$	Claimholders
Deductible	$\Longleftrightarrow$	Capital requirement

In an insurance contract, the insurance company leaves the first losses to the policyholder via a deductible. Reciprocally, the community of policyholders of an insurance company leaves the first insurance losses to shareholders by means of a capital requirement. In the next section, we describe the main purposes of deductibles in insurance contracts. Then, using this analogy with capital, we will offer rationales for capital requirements for insurance companies.

4.3 The Role of Deductibles in Insurance Contracts

There are three well-known reasons why deductibles are useful in insurance contracts.

(i) Transaction Costs

The settling of claims by an insurance company involves a number of administrative costs. The claim has to be filed, possible fraud by the policyholder has to be detected, and checks have to be processed. A well-known result by Arrow (1963) shows that an insurance contract with a deductible copes optimally with these costs. It is desirable to leave the "least risky" and most frequent part of the risk, namely the first losses, to the policyholder, because it saves the administrative costs that the company would otherwise incur in order to deal with this innocuous part of the risk. In other words, a contract with a deductible optimally trades off the benefit from risk transfer and the cost of settling claims.

(ii) Moral Hazard

For many insurable risks, the policyholder may partly control the distribution of losses. She may indeed exert more or less effort to limit the occurrence and/or cost of adverse events. In motor insurance, she may drive more or less carefully. In corporate insurance, a manufacturer may monitor whether the workforce complies with safety rules more or less closely. In many instances, this effort is impossible or prohibitively costly to observe by the insurance company, and comes at some cost for the policyholder (e.g., the cost in time of driving more slowly). This creates moral hazard. Indeed, if she purchases insurance, the policyholder no longer fully benefits from the positive consequences of such efforts, but she still bears the cost. As a result, she may exert less effort once insured so that purchasing insurance actually increases risk. A rational insurer should anticipate this opportunistic behavior and charge larger premiums. It is an inefficient situation: both the policyholder and the insurer would be better off with lower expected losses. Economic theory shows that, under fairly general assumptions, the optimal way to cope with this moral hazard problem is to include a deductible borne by the policyholder. This is the best *incentive* device. More precisely, among all the contractual arrangements that elicit effort from the policyholder, it is the one that minimizes the risk borne by the policyholder. In other words, the deductible is the optimal trade-off between the benefit from risk transfer and the need to provide the policyholder with incentives to "behave" by virtue of a residual risk exposure.

(iii) Adverse Selection

Moral hazard is an informational asymmetry between insurer and policyholder in which the *action* (typically, the choice of the intensity of the effort to reduce risk) of the latter is hidden from the former. Another form of informational asymmetry is hidden *information*. There are many instances in the insurance industry in which the policyholder has some information about her risk that the insurance company does not have. Again using motor insurance as an example, even though some observable characteristics (gender, age, track record of the driver, color of the car, etc.) help the insurance company guess whether the policyholder is a safe driver or not, it is difficult to observe the driver's risk characteristics fully. As a result, the insurer makes an "average" quote for each policyholder, which implies that good drivers subsidize bad drivers. But if this subsidy is too high, good drivers may refuse the deal, leading to a very inefficient market where only bad drivers are insured. Again, economic theory predicts that a deductible is the most efficient way of separating out good and bad risks by offering menus of contracts with different levels of deductible and different levels of premium. For example, bad drivers reveal themselves by accepting to pay a higher premium for a smaller deductible. It is preferable for them only if they expect many claims. Deductibles are a clever device that lead policyholders to self-select themselves, namely, choose a level of deductible that reveals their characteristics to the insurance company.

4.4 The Role of Insurance Capital to Mitigate Informational Problems

Now, let us revisit these three stories, replacing "insurer" by "policyholders," "policyholder" by "shareholders," and "deductible" by "capital requirements."

(i) Capital Requirements and Bankruptcy Costs

When the shareholders of an insurance company file for bankruptcy or declare that the assets of the company are insufficient to match the liabilities, then the policyholders, via their representatives, have to appoint a liquidator, who realizes the assets and fairly shares the proceeds between them. This liquidation is in general very costly. A capital requirement reduces the probability of bankruptcies occurring, and thus also reduces expected liquidation costs, which is socially desirable.

Insurance liquidations are very costly because a number of insurance assets become worthless or are significantly discounted as the company ceases to be a going concern. Claims on reinsurers or insurance intermediaries get more difficult to collect because these agents no longer have the prospect of profitable future business relationships as an incentive to meet their commitments in a timely fashion. Moreover, the proceeds from the fire sale of the least liquid assets (real estate, nonlisted securities) are in general below book values. In shallow capital markets (e.g., in continental European markets), even the most liquid securities may be sold under adverse conditions because of predatory trading.

(ii) Capital Requirements and Moral Hazard

We emphasized earlier that the inversion of the production cycle was an important source of informational asymmetry between the insiders (top management, inside shareholders) and the outsiders (mainly policyholders) of an insurance company. In particular, efficient loss mitigation by risk managers is something that is difficult to observe or contract upon, and may come at a private cost to insiders. With capital requirements, it becomes important for shareholders to make sure loss mitigation is carried out efficiently, because they have a significant stake in the outcome.

Viewing capital requirements as an incentive device sheds light on the explicit or implicit conditions that a firm willing to develop from scratch a new insurance portfolio must meet. In most countries, for the insurance license to be granted, it must be the case that some investors with financial expertise, typically other financial institutions, commit a significant stake in the first investment round. This ensures that some sophisticated investors will monitor the insurance company, because their stake is at risk. The appendix at the end of this chapter illustrates this point with an elementary model.

Moral hazard may also be part of the explanation of why the top management of Equitable did not implement any measure to deal with outstanding GARs in 1988, the time at which they stopped selling new GARs, which confirms that they were already aware of a potential danger. Equitable was a mutual. If it had instead been owned by sophisticated shareholders, these shareholders would have been concerned by the fact that GAR options were very likely to get in the money over a short horizon. Accordingly, they might have put some pressure on the top management to quickly renegotiate the contracts. ELAS instead waited until 1993, by which time such renegotiation turned out to be very painful.

Note, however, that using equity as an incentive device is pointless when moral hazard is driven by short-termism. Remember, for instance, that the GARs underwritten by Equitable in the 1960s did not imply any significant cash outflows for the first twenty years or so following the underwriting of the contracts. There are probably very few managers or share-holders who are concerned about the consequences of their decisions twenty years in the future.

(iii) Capital Requirements and Adverse Selection

Assume that there are several types of insurance risk manager. Some are good at their job, some are bad, but only share-holders, not the regulator, know their type. Capital structure is a device for separating them out, either by "signalling" or "screening."

"Signalling" means that the company may announce to the market that it is a "good" company by committing a sizable amount of capital. This is a credible announcement because a "bad" company would not take the risk of losing this cap-ital in a bankruptcy (the risk is larger for a bad company). To illustrate this signalling role of capital, note that Schroder Investment started selling its stake in Independent Insurance more than one year before the insurer filed for bankruptcy. This was a very interesting hint, meaning that this financially sophisticated investor was no longer willing to maintain its stake in the firm and signal its confidence in the management of Independent.

More relevant for prudential regulation is "screening." Pol-icyholders or their representatives may use capital regulation as a screening device. By refusing to purchase insurance from companies which do not meet the statutory level of capitaliza-tion, they screen companies: "bad" companies are not willing to operate because they have too much to lose by putting at risk the required amount of capital.

Note, however, that an equity stake is not the most effi-cient device for extracting shareholders' information. This is because a risky insurance company not only has a high prob-ability of failure, because of a mispriced portfolio, but also has some probability of huge profits, because of an aggres-sive investment strategy, for instance. The market valuation of equity takes into account the possible upside as well as the possible downside, so that the signal on the downside is scrambled by a signal on the upside. Policyholders are mainly concerned with the downside, however. In the banking literature, several scholars have noted that the price of *subordinated debt* is likely to deliver a purer signal about banks' probabilities of default than stock prices, because the prospects of a very high profit do not have much impact on the payoff to subordinated creditors—only default probability does. As a result, some authors (see, for example, Calomiris 1998; Bliss 2001) have suggested that requiring a minimum level of traded subordinated debt within the capital requirements of banks would help the regulator extract information from capital markets. This is an appealing idea. It seems of limited practical interest, however, for insurance companies. Only a few of them, the largest groups, have capital needs that are large enough to maintain a liquid market for subordinated bonds at a reasonable cost.

4.5 Conclusion: The Inversion of the Production Cycle Creates Agency Problems That Can Be Mitigated by Capital Requirements for Insurance Companies

Applying capital structure theory, we have clarified the reasons why the capitalization of insurance companies matters. To sum up, capital structure matters for any firm as soon as the corporate game is plagued by some agency problem. This is very likely to be the case for insurance companies, because their production cycle is inverted and stretched over time. As a result, it is important that insurance companies be sufficiently capitalized in order to be run efficiently.

But because neither shareholders nor policyholders have the right incentives to include a capital structure covenant in the insurance contract, this has to be enforced by external regulation. Policyholders cannot enforce such a rule: because of a collective-action problem, they cannot behave as a unique, tough claimholder. Dealing with the absence of a tough claimholder is the scope of the next chapter.

4.6 Appendix: Capital Requirements as an Incentive Device

This appendix contains a simple reinterpretation, in the context of insurance, of the basic model in Holmström and Tirole (1997). Let us consider the following situation. A group of institutional investors contemplate starting up an insurance company. The statutory capital requirement is I. For simplicity, the risk profile of the portfolio is as follows. It may either deliver a final profit R or a huge loss, larger than the capital requirement, hence leading the company to bankruptcy. Here, the statutory capital requirement is meant as a buffer to limit the extent of losses borne by claimholders.

There is a moral hazard problem: the probability of success of the company depends on the managers' efforts. By monitoring these managers, the founders of the company, who are institutional investors with financial and insurance expertise, can increase the probability of success by δp. We denote by p the probability of success if they exert monitoring.[4] However, this monitoring effort involves time and resources. It comes at a private cost c to them. The monitoring effort cannot be observed by the regulator. The initial amount of capital that founders can invest in the firm is A. It is assumed that

$$pR - c > I > (p - \delta p)R.$$

Under what conditions are the founders able to start up the company? If $A \geqslant I$, they have enough capital to meet the statutory requirement and the above inequality ensures that they will monitor the managers. Indeed, their project has a positive net present value only if they monitor. Now, if $A < I$ they

---

[4] The probability of success in the absence of monitoring is thus $(p - \delta p)$.

have to tap outside investors to finance the difference $I - A$. Outside investors have no ability to monitor the operations, and they are willing to put some money into the project only if they have some hope of breaking even. Outside investors can break even only if insiders monitor the company, otherwise the above inequality implies that the project has a negative net present value. Insiders have an incentive to monitor only if their stake in the positive outcome, denoted R_I, is such that

$$pR_I - c > (p - \delta p)R_I.$$

This inequality means that monitoring, although costly, is more profitable to them. So the stake of insiders must satisfy the inequality

$$R_I > \frac{c}{\delta p}.$$

At the same time, the expected return for outside investors must be positive:

$$p(R - R_I) \geqslant I - A.$$

Combining these two inequalities shows that the firm is able to start up only if

$$A > I - p\left(R - \frac{c}{\delta p}\right).$$

Because of moral hazard, the insurance company can start up only if the sophisticated shareholders have a sufficient initial stake in it.

5

Absence of a Tough Claimholder in the Financial Structure of Insurance Companies and Incomplete Contracts

5.1   Absence of a Tough Claimholder

The inversion of the production cycle may give rise to a chain reaction in which poor governance and value destruction reinforce each other because of the absence of a tough, sophisticated claimholder within insurance companies. A typical nonfinancial firm has two sorts of claimholder who possess financial expertise, or who can afford to hire experts: large shareholders and banks. Banks play an important role if a negative shock hits the firm, because they are concerned by the possibility of not recovering the full value of their loans if the situation deteriorates further. More importantly, unlike shareholders they have less incentive to bet for resurrection. To see this, assume that a firm's net wealth is reduced by, say, 60% by a negative shock. Shareholders have already lost a lot of their initial investment, namely 60%. Taking a very risky bet that results either in a large bankruptcy, with a high probability, or a huge profit, with a small probability, is appealing to them. Because of their limited liability, they have a large appetite for risk. Losing the residual 40% may be offset by the prospect of a large upside, even with a low probability of success. Conversely, banks have the incentive to take prompt corrective action which stabilizes earnings so as to preserve the full value of their claims. This is because their claims are senior to equity. Projects with a large downside and a large upside are not appealing to them, because they do not benefit much from the upside.

Unlike in nonfinancial firms, the holders of senior claims within insurance companies are not sophisticated investors such as banks, but simply the policyholders themselves. Their stake represents a large fraction of the right-hand side of the balance sheet, typically around 90%: insurance companies are highly leveraged firms. This high leverage creates strong incentives for shareholders to move toward risk-shifting policies. Moreover, unlike banks, policyholders are dispersed and insufficiently informed; none of them (individually) has enough incentive to spend time, energy, and/or financial resources to monitor the management of her insurance company. Policyholders face a fundamental free-riding problem. We develop this point, formalized by Dewatripont and Tirole (1994), in this chapter. We view this as the main justification for the existence of a prudential authority. This does not mean that this authority should strive for a complete elimination of failures. Failures are an essential element of economic life by which inefficient firms are eliminated and assets are reassigned to more-efficient firms. Moreover, they constitute by themselves a powerful disciplining device for managers, who can sometimes be tempted to enjoy private benefits of control or build inefficient empires. Of course failures are *ex post* costly, and typically exert negative externalities on the firm's creditors, staff, and customers, which explains why resolution methods have to be designed carefully, in order to limit those externalities while maintaining incentives for managers and stockholders. But aiming at zero failure is unrealistic, since it would imply either that insurers stop taking risks (which would mean abandoning their core business), or that solvency requirements are huge, which would make financial services prohibitively costly. Therefore, it is important to determine when prudential supervisors have to intervene (this is the role of solvency requirements) and which resolution method has to be employed when an insurance company has to be reorganized.

It is interesting to note that there are some situations in the insurance industry in which the policyholders do not face this coordination problem. It is so, for instance, when a large and sophisticated broker, like Aon or Marsh & McLennan, contracts with the company on behalf of policyholders. Very interestingly, in the absence of any regulation, such brokers stop underwriting business with companies whose credit rating is downgraded below a given threshold. They could instead ask a lower insurance premium as a compensation for an increase in default risk, but perhaps because they are concerned with an agency problem, they just stop doing business with poorly capitalized firms. In other words, when the policyholders are represented by a large and sophisticated broker, and thus do not face a collective-action problem, the outcome of free markets is somewhat similar to a regulatory capital requirement.

In practice, prudential authorities do more than brokers: not only do they monitor whether insurers comply with capital adequacy rules, but they are also supposed to make important decisions, about reorganization or even liquidation of the insurance companies that have breached these rules, for example. To analyze these transfers of control rights from shareholders to the regulator, we need a theory of capital structure in which such rights matter in the first place. We have overlooked this point so far because we have invoked theories based only on *cash flow rights*. More precisely, we have stressed that because debt and equity imply claims of different seniorities on the cash flows generated by the assets of the firm, an inappropriate mix of debt and equity distorts incentives to produce effort or reveal private information. In practice, debt and equity differ not only with respect to cash flow rights, but also with respect to *control rights*. In principle, equity-holders have control over the firm, i.e., they are in charge of making all the important decisions, as long as the firm's net wealth is sufficiently high. Debtholders (in particular banks) exert these control rights whenever the firm becomes insolvent or even gets close to insolvency. They become the most important decision makers when the firm has to be restructured or liquidated. From a theoretical standpoint, it is not obvious at first sight why control rights should matter. Everybody understands that a firm has to be restructured whenever its indebtedness reaches a certain threshold. This could simply be written down in the corporate contract and implemented by the management once this threshold is hit, regardless of who is in control of the firm when this occurs. But because contracts are inherently incomplete, i.e., because it is too difficult to describe *ex ante* all the relevant actions that might need to be taken in case of future distress, the identity of the agent in charge in a time of distress does matter.

5.2 Prudential Regulation and Incomplete Contracts

The reason that control rights matter has been identified in recent developments in corporate-finance and contract theory, pioneered in particular by Aghion and Bolton (1992) and by Hart (1988).[1] This reason is generically referred to as *incompleteness of contracts*. Incompleteness of contracts means that the course of action that has to be taken under some future circumstances cannot be precisely described in a contract, because either the actions or the circumstances are too difficult to figure out and describe in advance. In the latter case,

---

[1] A thorough account of the implications of contract incompleteness for the financial structure of firms can be found in Hart (1995).

the situation is one of "noncontractible information," while the former case is defined as one of "noncontractible action."

Noncontractible Information

The accounting information provided by a firm is necessary to assess its financial health, but it is certainly not sufficient, since it is a very simplified, standardized summary of its actual situation. The opinion one may have about a complex organization like a large corporation is a result of a combination of a large number of other pieces of information, regarding for instance the general environment of the firm, or the personality of its top management. This is particularly true for an industry with a long (and inverted) production cycle, like insurance. To forecast the evolution of an insurance portfolio, one has to make guesses about the evolution of such complex factors as global terrorism, changes in climate, court decisions regarding professional liability, long-run returns on stock markets, etc. As a result, the way in which an expert, despite being endowed with strong quantitative skills, assesses the overall situation of an insurance company is ultimately by "gut feeling" more than the outcome of some well-defined computations. A gut feeling is a good example of noncontractible information. It is an idea that one finds convincing but cannot fully justify. Therefore, it can hardly be incorporated into a contract since it is very difficult to communicate credibly to a third party for verification purposes.

Noncontractible Actions

Even if one assumes that some contractible piece of information, like very bad financial ratios, makes restructuring of the company necessary, it is still likely to be the case that the detail of what has to be done cannot be contracted upon. As the old business saying goes, "Management is more art than science." How to cut costs? What should the new underwriting criteria be? Which assets have to be sold quickly? Which ones must be carried to wait for better "market conditions"? Which bargaining strategy should be used with reinsurers? A restructuring policy cannot be derived from an algorithm or some systematic decision-making rule. Two different managers would implement it in two different ways.

Because a number of actions and pieces of information, in particular the most crucial ones, can typically not be described in detail in the corporate contract, control rights matter, or more precisely *residual control rights*. Residual control rights encompass the control over all factors that cannot be described in contracts. By definition, the owner of such rights has crucial discretionary powers. Therefore, it is very important to make sure she is the appropriate decision maker. Viewed through the lenses of contract incompleteness, corporate governance is the mechanism by which residual control rights over the firm are granted to the right agent at the right time.

5.3 The "Representation Hypothesis"

Following Dewatripont and Tirole (1994), we shall now apply this broad idea to the regulation of insurance companies. A formal model is outside the scope of this book. However, technically oriented readers can check that it can be easily adapted from chapters 7 and 8 of Dewatripont and Tirole (1994). The formal analysis developed by Dewatripont and Tirole may be summarized as follows. For simplicity, we consider that there are only two ways to run an insurance company: a "safe" strategy and a "risky" one. The risky strategy encompasses, for instance, commercial development at a fast pace, aggressive underwriting, diversification in new business lines or new markets, exposure to "exotic" financial risks. With the safe strategy, we have in mind stabilizing the portfolio: sticking to a core business and restricting investments to listed stocks and high-grade bonds. We assume that these strategies are not contractible. This captures the fact that there is in practice a vast, continuous spectrum of strategies from the riskiest to the safest that cannot be described in detail in any contract. We also assume that the information available to shareholders and policyholders regarding the financial and operational situation of the company has a simple structure. People receive "bad news" or "good news." Again, this binary signal is meant to make the point clear. It is assumed to be only partially contractible. In practice, people process a vast flow of information and derive an overall impression which is arguably difficult to use as a legal trigger. However, part of this information, in particular public accounts, can be contracted upon. We then make the following natural assumption on the optimal way to run the company. It is optimal to undertake the "risky" strategy when the news about the company is good. If risks are under control, operations profitable, and the environment appropriate, the right thing to do is to keep developing the company. Conversely, if news is bad, the company should be restructured and it should focus on restoring the profitability of its core business.

Because neither information nor action are contractible, corporate governance matters. Namely, residual control rights over the insurance company have to be allocated in such a way that these optimal decisions are made. This is possible because policyholders and shareholders have different views. We have already mentioned that, because of limited liability, shareholders are biased toward risky actions. They benefit fully from the upside while limiting their stake in the downside. Conversely, current policyholders do not care much about the firm's profits. They are mainly concerned about their claims not being settled if the risky action turns bad, thus they have an objective interest in a safe choice. This is why it is optimal to leave residual control rights to the shareholders in times of good news and to the policyholders in times of bad news. Due to their respective biases, they will indeed implement the optimal decision in each case. The trigger of such control rights allocation can only be the contractible part of the signal, namely accounting information. As a result, the value of the firm is maximized *ex ante* if the governance rules ensure that holders of "tough" claims, policyholders in the case of insurance companies, are being granted control in times of bad news, namely when the firm becomes undercapitalized, while shareholders are left free to decide and implement the strategy otherwise. As already mentioned, the community of policyholders cannot exert control rights in practice. This is why a prudential authority has a role to play, *as the representative of the current holders of outstanding insurance claims in the governance structure of insurance companies.*

We view this "representation hypothesis" formulated by Dewatripont and Tirole (1994) as the essential justification for prudential regulation in the insurance industry. The prudential regulator should ideally behave like the "banker" of insurance companies, playing the role of a tough claimholder checking and balancing the power of shareholders in bad times, and therefore reproducing the governance system of nonfinancial firms. To emphasize this role of prudential regulation as an optimal corporate governance mechanism, it is interesting to stress the striking similarity between prudential ratios on the one hand, and loan covenants characterizing the relationship between, say, a large bank and a small industrial firm on the other. In order to protect their interests, commercial banks include provisions in their loan covenants such as maximal debt-to-asset ratio, minimal liquidity ratio, and collateral seizure when such ratios are not met. This sounds broadly similar to prudential regulation as we have defined it in chapter 3 of this book.

Drawing on the theoretical developments of chapters 4 and 5, we are now equipped to outline policy recommendations that are consistent with this view of prudential regulation as a substitute for governance.

6

How to Organize the Regulation of Insurance Companies

We have argued that the prudential authority should behave as the "banker" of insurance companies. Just as banks screen and monitor their debtors, the prudential authority should screen and monitor insurance firms, without intervening in their ongoing operations as long as simple and easily verifiable financial ratios are met. But it should be committed to making prompt and tough decisions as soon as a company no longer complies with certain prudential rules. When this happens, the only aim of the regulator must be the recovery of *current* policyholders' outstanding claims, even if it hurts future business opportunities or is detrimental to the workforce and shareholders. From this simple principle, we derive six policy recommendations for the organization of the prudential regulation of insurance companies.

6.1 Simple Prudential Ratios

> Prudential ratios should be defined simply and derived from public accounts, because these accounts are easily verifiable.

We have mentioned that, given the current state of the art in financial economics and actuarial science, it is unrealistic to assume that any "one-size-fits-all" ratio, even a very high-tech one, is likely to predict insurance failures. An alternative solution would be to rely on the internal models developed by insurance companies. These models are likely to be more reliable because they are calibrated with more idiosyncratic information. This is the route taken by the Basel Committee for the so-called Basel II reform of banking supervision. However, we think this has an important drawback. Such models are black boxes that only a limited number of "rocket scientists" can open and understand. It makes them barely verifiable. Because we view prudential ratios as legal drivers of control rights allocation rather than "scientific" determinants of the "right" amount of capital, we think that verifiability is crucial. This is necessary to make sure that the prudential authority intervenes in a timely fashion if it has to. It is also the only way to punish it *ex post* if it failed to intervene. Entering into the details of the definition of the ratio is beyond the scope of this book, but what we have in mind is a compromise between the overly simple European Solvency Margin and the unnecessarily complex American Risk Based Capital. Of course, we keep in mind that prudential ratios that do not fully reflect the market's assessment of risks have a cost. They may imply regulatory arbitrage, i.e., distorted and inefficient underwriting and/or asset management choices. The "double trigger" regulation we propose below should mitigate this adverse effect to a large extent.

Finally, note that commercial banks do in general write down very simple ratios in their loans covenants. They could easily set up high-tech formulas. There is no doubt that the relevant expertise is available in-house. The reason they use very simple triggers instead is probably the same as the reason we put forward: banks need covenants that can be easily and quickly verified, because prompt action is the first-order concern when one of their customers experiences financial distress.

6.2 "Double Trigger"

In the spirit of the gradual approach set up in the United States, we propose "double trigger" regulation with two levels of capital requirements. In such a system, three situations are possible. If an insurance company satisfies the first (and highest) capital requirement, then the scope of regulatory intervention must be limited to making sure that the firm's reports are correct and based upon sincere information. If this first threshold is hit, the prudential authority must carry out further investigations and establish with the firm a plan to restore its prudential situation. Finally, if the situation deteriorates further or if these investigations reveal additional losses, so that the second (lower) threshold is hit, then the prudential authority must transfer the case to a guarantee fund run by the industry, whose role is detailed below. In this case, the regulator and the guarantee fund jointly take over control rights.

The role of the first threshold is to protect shareholders and the top management against a regulatory bias toward excessive interventionism. This is consistent with our claim that regulatory intervention in well-functioning and well-capitalized firms is counterproductive. Shareholders are the best decision makers in this case and the threat of regulatory interference reduces managerial incentives toward innovation and operational efficiency. As a result, the regulator should intervene for verification purposes only above this threshold—neither being granted any kind of control rights nor being given entitlement to make specific management recommendations. Note that the scope of regulation above this verification threshold is limited but nevertheless absolutely crucial. Remember that one of the reasons why financially constrained insurance companies may end up spectacularly insolvent is because underreserving is easy and tempting. This underreserving is something that is difficult to detect by auditing firms because there is no clear-cut definition of what appropriate reserves are. As a result, we think that the top priority for the regulator, above the first threshold, is to evaluate firms' reserving policies and detect changes in these policies by looking carefully at the runoff triangles.[1]

When this first threshold is hit, the prudential authority is being granted rights, as well as duties. Namely, it must carry out detailed investigations and, based upon the results, validate a plan proposed by the firm to restore its solvency. This constraint is meant to provide the regulator with a strong incentive to intervene effectively and promptly, because it provides an unambiguous basis for posterior sanctions.

When the second threshold is hit, we introduce, in addition to shareholders and the prudential authority, a third player endowed with control rights, i.e., a guarantee fund run by representatives of the industry. The motivation for this proposal is explained below in section 6.4.

On the whole, such a gradual approach should mitigate the inefficiencies inherent in regulatory capital requirements. If a firm does not comply with the first threshold but has clearly identified the reason for the noncompliance and has the situation under control, it should quickly be able to provide the prudential authority with evidence of a satisfactory plan for restoring its situation without any dramatic change in its strategy. Creating a "gray area" between the first and second thresholds, where shareholders and the prudential authority share control rights, is a pragmatic proposal. This proposal

---

[1] Runoff triangles are tables that sort the payments of each past financial year according to the years in which the underlying contracts were underwritten. For instance, the entry on row 1990 and column 8 of a runoff triangle shows the payments that a company made in the year 1998 for the claims deriving from contracts underwritten in the year 1990. By comparing these figures with the firm's past reserves, it is possible to identify a company's tendency to underreserve or overreserve at the various stages of the evolution of a claim, and therefore to assess the current reserves.

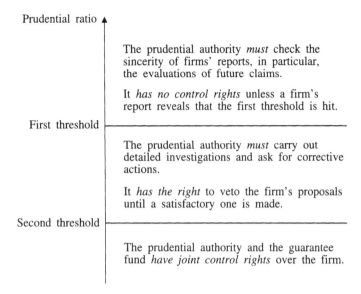

Prudential ratio

The prudential authority *must* check the sincerity of firms' reports, in particular, the evaluations of future claims.

It *has no control rights* unless a firm's report reveals that the first threshold is hit.

First threshold

The prudential authority *must* carry out detailed investigations and ask for corrective actions.

It *has the right* to veto the firm's proposals until a satisfactory one is made.

Second threshold

The prudential authority and the guarantee fund *have joint control rights* over the firm.

Figure 6.1.   The "double-trigger" prudential system.

aims to account for the fact that analyzing the situation of an insurance company is a difficult job, where even well-trained professionals are likely to make mistakes. This area plays the role of a buffer that grants additional time to shareholders and the regulator to correct such mistakes. Figure 6.1 summarizes this "double-trigger' structure.

6.3   An Independent but Accountable Prudential Authority

> The prudential authority should be given a clear agenda (namely implementing the two-triggered supervision system suggested above) and shielded from political pressure. However, it should be audited by parliament on a regular basis to check *ex post* that the mandatory actions described in its agenda have been taken.

In the system that we advocate, the role of the prudential authority is thus threefold: verify the accounts of all insurers; watch the companies with a solvency margin below the first threshold more closely; and liquidate those with a solvency margin below the second threshold. But liquidation decisions are seldom optimal from an *ex post* point of view, especially if one takes into account the interests of shareholders, managers, and employees, who can lobby the government to bail out the distressed firm with taxpayers' money. This is why it is important to shield the prudential authority from any form of political pressure. However, independence cannot work without accountability. This is why *ex post* control of the prudential authority has to be organized, for assessing its performance on a regular basis.

We suggest that parliament carries out such evaluations, for instance in the middle and at the end of the tenure of the regulator. This assessment should be eased by the "double trigger" system, featuring simply verifiable thresholds and mandatory actions to be taken by the regulator.

6.4 Granting Control Rights to the Industry via a Guarantee Fund

> A guarantee fund should be set up, providing policyholders with insurance against their insurer's default. The fund should raise premiums and capital from insurance companies: it must be owned and run by the industry. Moreover, as already mentioned, the fund should be given control rights in insurance companies that fail to meet the second capital requirement.

Most countries have created guarantee funds indemnifying policyholders whose insurance company defaults. Such funds are widespread in life insurance. In property/casualty insurance, their scope is sometimes restricted to mandatory insurance such as motor liability. The rationale for the creation of such funds is that, if the fund is properly designed, the benefit from pooling default risk overcomes the moral hazard that may result from the fact that policyholders lose the incentive to monitor their insurer. But such funds are also desirable for a completely different reason. They are very good candidates for playing the role of "tough claimholder" that is missing from insurance companies and which we identified as the market failure justifying intervention in insurance markets. By construction, the interests of this fund are perfectly congruent with current policyholders' interests: the consequence of a company's failure is transferred from the latter to the former. We advocate that this fund should be a private corporation, raising equity from private investors and risk-based insurance premiums from insurance companies. Moreover, it should be granted control rights, along with the prudential authority, over insurance companies who fail to meet the "second trigger," namely the least demanding prudential ratio. If the fund is sufficiently well-capitalized, then its management and shareholders should have the perfect incentives to be tough and liquidate firms when needed, in order to maximize the recovery value of outstanding insurance claims. It amounts to minimizing their production costs! Moreover, its directors being representatives of the industry, they may contemplate additional benefits from a liquidation: elimination of a competitor and limitation of the negative externalities exerted on them by a large failure (reputational loss for the insurance industry as a whole). On the whole, such a private fund has all the features of the "insurers' banker" that is missing in the corporate structure of insurance companies. The reason that we still find it useful to leave joint control rights to the prudential authority, even when the second threshold is hit, is that, depending upon local market structures, there may also be a collusion problem. The top management and the directors of different firms may find it worthwhile to be lenient with each other in order to live a quiet life. The role of the prudential authority would be to prevent such opportunistic behavior.

6.5 A Single Accounting Standard

> Reports to the prudential authority and public disclosure should build upon the same accounting standards. This is not to deny that regulatory reports may feature more detailed information, but the primary evaluation rules must be the same, e.g., either historical cost or marked-to-market in both cases.

We have stressed throughout the book that, because of the nature of their claims, policyholders and shareholders have a natural disagreement on corporate strategies, the former being more conservative than the latter. In order to deal with this misalignment, some countries, including the United States, have introduced different accounting rules for regulatory and public reports. The regulatory rules are of course more conservative. We do not think this is a good idea. The consequence is that the top management of insurance companies has to be bilingual, speaking the GAAP (Generally Accepted Accounting Principles—the standards used for public accounts) language with shareholders and the SAP (Statutory Accounting Principles—the standards used for supervisory reports) language with the regulator. But if one views the prudential regulator as the representative of the policyholders, and as such, one of the stakeholders fully involved in the corporate governance of insurance companies, this adds a lot of confusion. In particular in the "gray area" between the two solvency thresholds, in which shareholders and policyholders have to find a compromise based upon analyses provided by the management, it seems much more preferable to have everybody speaking the same language.

In practice, we believe that the regulator should be content with the public accounting standards, and not impose the production of another layer of reports based on more conservative regulatory standards. We find it highly undesirable that insurance accounting rules be determined by the prudential regulator. This creates a real risk of fossilizing accounting standards by preventing the innovations that naturally take place in a free market for auditing services.

6.6   Limiting the Scope of Prudential Regulation

> It is not desirable to have the prudential authority supervising the whole insurance production line, including not only insurers but also brokers downstream and reinsurance companies upstream. The scope of prudential regulation should be restricted to primary insurance companies and insurance groups.

As illustrated, for instance, by the balance sheets of Independent Insurance presented in chapter 2, a significant fraction of the assets of insurance companies are claims to insurance intermediaries (e.g., brokers) and reinsurance companies. This is because insurance companies are in the middle of the insurance "production line," between insurance intermediaries in charge of acquiring customers downstream and reinsurance companies bearing the most extreme parts of the risk upstream. Several countries have drawn the conclusion that the solvency of an insurance company is determined by the quality of these claims, and have decided to extend supervision to reinsurers and brokers as a result. We do not think that this is a good idea. Regarding reinsurance supervision, the question of whether it is desirable or not is irrelevant: efficient supervision of reinsurance companies is just not feasible in practice. The reinsurance market is a global one. Sensible supervision of professional reinsurers could only be carried out by an integrated, global agency—it is out of range of fragmented national entities. The job of supervising brokers is very different from insurance supervision. Brokers are pure intermediaries, thus they are not exposed to any significant asset liability mismatch risk. The main point of supervision of brokers is to prevent a crook from running away with insurance premiums! This is not a very technical job, but it is very time-consuming and would create an exponential increase in the cost of supervision if carried out seriously.

A much more efficient and economical way to deal with reinsurers' and brokers' default risk is to create sufficient incentives for insurance companies to actively manage this risk themselves. Imposing sufficiently strict conditions under which claims on reinsurers and brokers may qualify as assets in the computation of the company's prudential ratio creates such incentives. For instance, the qualification may depend upon the credit rating of the issuers of claims. Another way of implementing this, and in our opinion a much safer way, is to admit only the fraction of these claims that is collateralized by reinsurers and brokers, the collateral being treated as part of the company's assets for the purpose of computing its prudential ratios. With this constraint, shareholders and the top management, if they are not willing to give up control rights, fully internalize this need to monitor reinsurers' and brokers' solvencies. Having ongoing business relationships with them, they are likely to be much better informed than the regulator, and thus perform this task more efficiently.

6.7 What if This Is Not Enough?

To be fair, some of these recommendations are already being applied, at least partly, in several prudential systems. We view these basic rules as the minimal package required to practically implement our approach of prudential regulation as a replication of sound corporate governance.

As mentioned at the beginning of the book, regulation is desirable only if the costs of regulation are smaller than the benefits from mitigating a market failure. While we believe that the regulatory design that we offer is an improvement over the existing regulations, we agree that whether such a system of regulation is better than no regulation at all is ultimately an empirical question. In order to ensure that the theoretical design that we offer is preferable to laissez faire in practice, prudential regulation should be on a *voluntary* basis (see Morrison (2004) for an alternative motive for voluntary insurance regulation). Insurance companies should be free to operate without being subject to prudential regulation, provided, of course, that they make it very clear to the public that they are doing so. Then, if regulation maximizes the social value of insurance even after regulatory costs, firms that decide to subject themselves to regulation should be more competitive and should be preferred by policyholders. Conversely, regulated firms would be driven out of business by competing unregulated firms.

In the next two chapters, we go beyond the exposition of these general rules, and further discuss their fit with the environment of insurance companies. First, we argue that reinsurers perform a function that complements insurance supervision. Second, we discuss the interplay of these rules with the regulation of financial conglomerates, and with the regulatory management of systemic risk.

7

The Role of Reinsurance

While describing the role of capital structure in chapters 4 and 5, we have stressed that corporations design various securities, such as debt and equity, in order to optimally split risks among their various claimholders. Alternatively, they can also insulate their claimholders from some risks by hedging these risks. Namely, they can immunize the cash flows they promise to their claimholders against some risks by purchasing insurance from a third party who has a better ability to bear these risks.

Insurance companies, like other firms, also have the ability to purchase insurance against the risks generated by their core activities. In the insurance industry, this operation is termed reinsurance. The sellers of protection are the reinsurers. The insurance contracts between the primary insurer and its reinsurers are referred to as a reinsurance treaties. After briefly describing the organization of the reinsurance market, we argue that reinsurance operations generate a lot of useful information that should be systematically and carefully processed by prudential supervisors.

7.1 Organization of the Reinsurance Market

Reinsurance is a very important feature of the non-life-insurance business. In 2004, direct insurers have ceded business worth $167.8 billion worldwide. This corresponds to an average cession rate of 6% (Group of Thirty 2006).[1] The cession rate is the ratio

$$\frac{\text{Ceded premiums}}{\text{Gross premiums}},$$

where the ceded premiums are the premiums paid by the insurers to their reinsurers for their protection, and the gross premiums are the total premiums earned by the insurers in primary insurance markets. Thus, the cession rate is a measure of the fraction of the risks that insurers retrade in the reinsurance market.

Reinsurance is to some extent reminiscent of securitization for lending institutions. Both mechanisms allow financial institutions to resell in a secondary market the risks that they have originated. The reinsurance market has a very specific structure, however: it has a "pyramidal" organization. The generic reinsurance treaty involves two sorts of specialized player: a primary or direct insurer on the one hand, and professional reinsurers on the other. The primary insurer cedes part of the risk she underwrites on the primary market to the professional reinsurers, whose purpose is to accept such secondary risks, but who do not carry out any direct business. This is not to deny that some risk transfer between direct insurers also takes place, but the bulk of reinsurance transactions comply with this pattern: according to Swiss Re (1998) estimations, the reinsurance business is dominated by specialized reinsurance companies. Professional reinsurers provide more than 80% of global reinsurance capacity, the top four companies providing around 30% of it.

---

[1] Global data on reinsurance are somewhat scarce, partly because of the over-the-counter nature of deals and partly because it is difficult to disentangle actual risk transfers from internal reinsurance, aiming mainly at tax and regulatory arbitrage within insurance groups. These figures have been provided to the Group of Thirty by Swiss Re Economic Research & Consulting, considered to be one of the most reliable sources within the industry.

Interestingly, despite the absence of any regulatory constraint, most reinsurance treaties have a standard design. Treaties fall into two categories: proportional and nonproportional reinsurance.

The so-called proportional reinsurance treaties (quota-share treaties or surplus treaties) rest on the following principle:

$$\frac{\text{Ceded premiums}}{\text{Gross premiums}} = \frac{\text{Ceded claims}}{\text{Gross claims}}.$$

Thus, the ceding company and the reinsurers share the same loss ratio, but of course not the same combined ratio[2] because their operational expenses are different. More precisely, in such treaties the reinsurers typically pay a reinsurance commission to the ceding insurer. This is meant to compensate for the fact that the insurer still bears all the administrative and acquisition costs associated with the whole portfolio, while she gives the fraction of the ceded premiums meant to face these costs to the reinsurer. We now introduce some notation:

- g is the primary insurer's ratio of expenses per dollar of collected premiums;

- c is the reinsurance commission rate (commission per dollar of ceded premium);

- a is the cession rate (the ratio of ceded premiums over gross premiums);

- r_{net} and r_{gross} are the returns earned by the insurer on each dollar of premium after and before reinsurance, respectively;

- S and P are gross losses and gross premiums.

---

[2] The combined ratio features the costs of claims plus management costs minus financial products in the numerator and premiums in the denominator.

We obtain

$$r_{\text{net}} = (1 - a) \times \left(1 - \frac{S + gP}{P}\right) + a(c - g)$$

$$= (1 - a) \times r_{\text{gross}} + a(c - g).$$

Thus, the combined ratio net of reinsurance, r_{net}, is smaller than the gross combined ratio r_{gross} if and only if the commission rate is smaller than the expense ratio: $c < g$.

Nonproportional treaties (excess of loss, aggregate loss, stop loss) are very similar to insurance contracts with a deductible and a limited extent. The treaty carefully defines the underlying potential losses that it covers. It may apply to each loss deriving from each single policy in a given portfolio or to the aggregate amount of losses deriving from a given portfolio over a given period and/or due to a given event (e.g., a hurricane or a terrorist attack). For instance, an A XS B excess-of-loss treaty in motor insurance means that for each claim deriving from a car insurance policy, the reinsurers will pay up to \$$A$ after a deductible ("priority" in reinsurance terminology) of \$$B$. In financial terms, the payoff of an A XS B nonproportional layer is equivalent to the payoff resulting from a long position on a call with strike B and a short position on a call with strike $B + A$ written on the underlying losses. In general, a nonproportional cover is split into several (between two and ten) excess-of-loss treaties that decompose the total protection into layers of increasing priorities.

In addition to these traditional treaties, so-called "financial reinsurance" treaties have grown significantly over the last fifteen years and have been at the heart of some recent corporate scandals. These treaties are much less standardized, and describing their various forms would take us too long, but the main motivation behind them may be summarized as follows. Broadly speaking, the reinsurer grants to the ceding company a loan of face value equal to the estimation of a given set of outstanding claims. As a result, the ceding company is hedged against liquidity risk. The uncertainty about the date at which claims will have to be settled is no longer a concern for her provided the loan has a sufficiently long maturity. However, she stills bears the runoff risk, namely the risk that the final settlement value will be smaller or larger than its initial estimate. Financial reinsurance is a form of liquidity insurance. It aims at fully transferring the timing risk to reinsurers, leaving the runoff risk to the ceding company. Some of these structures have become quite contentious lately—roughly speaking because some ceding companies have tried to exploit the complex nature of the deal to avoid booking the reimbursement of the loan as a liability.

Reinsurance and capital are substitutes. More precisely, insurance companies can decide to sell the risks that policyholders or their representatives do not want to bear either to their financiers, by means of capital, or to professional reinsurers via reinsurance treaties. This is documented by Garven and Lamm-Tennant (2003), who find that reinsurance demand increases with financial leverage. In other words, firms with high leverage compensate for the fact that they have a small capital buffer against the fluctuations of their insurance losses by reducing these fluctuations with the purchase of reinsurance. Firms tend to have an integrated risk-management approach in which they coordinate their use of capital and reinsurance. Consistent with this is the fact that in most systems of prudential regulation (e.g., Risk Based Capital in the United States or the Solvency Margin system in Europe), the minimum capital requirement is explicitly reduced by reinsurance purchase. Another piece of anecdotal evidence in support of this point is the fact that the so-called contracts of *bottomry*, which were the prevailing form of reinsurance in Italy in fourteenth century, consisted in *ex ante* financing the repayment of which was conditioned by the absence of loss. The risk-management and financing sides of the operation were not disentangled.

Now, on what grounds do insurers make the decision to tap reinsurance for some risks, in particular the most volatile, and capital markets for the others? In other words, what is the specific ability of reinsurers that makes them the most competitive bearers of some types of risk? The most widespread answer is that reinsurers are more diversified than primary insurers. They do not rely on a particular distribution network and they underwrite all over the world in many business lines. This makes them less risk averse than direct insurers, who have more concentrated risk exposures. There is no doubt that this well-known rationale for reinsurance is relevant for some risks, such as natural catastrophes. However, an empirical finding from Mayers and Smith (1990) suggests that imperfect diversification does not seem to be the main determinant of reinsurance demand. Within a sample of U.S. insurance companies, they find that less-diversified firms, either geographically or across business lines, demand less reinsurance. Of course this does not support the view of reinsurance as a diversification device.

A justification for reinsurance that we find more consistent with empirical evidence is as follows. Reinsurers have a very high level of expertise in risk management. Research departments are much larger within reinsurance firms than within insurance companies. In particular, reinsurers are experts in dealing with the extreme realizations of risks. Large, catastrophic losses represent business-as-usual for them, while they are, by definition, rare, unusual events for primary insurers and their financiers. By contracting with reinsurers, primary insurers can benefit from this expertise. Reinsurers provide real services in risk management to ceding companies. The findings from Mayers and Smith (1990) that less-diversified insurers demand less reinsurance is consistent with this: highly focused insurers are more likely to develop the required expertise for their business in-house.

Moreover, thanks to this expertise, reinsurers are able to monitor risk management and loss mitigation carried out by primary insurers. They actually have strong incentives to monitor because it drives the profitability of reinsurance treaties. Doherty and Smetters (2005) find evidence that reinsurers play a role in loss mitigation within insurance companies, either by monitoring ceding companies or by designing efficient dynamic contracts (experience rating). This monitoring of insurers by reinsurers is important, because it "certifies" the management of insurance companies vis-à-vis outsiders. It reduces the moral hazard problem between insurance companies and their outside shareholders. The latter are indeed reassured by the presence of sophisticated reinsurers, who send a credible signal about the quality of the firm's portfolio. They commit credibly to monitor future loss mitigation by having a stake in the outcome via reinsurance treaties. It is as if rating agencies were buying bonds from the rated entities in order to signal to the market that their ratings are credible.

This theory of reinsurance as informed financing provides more satisfactory predictions than the diversification theory. If diversification was the main rationale for reinsurance, then insurance companies would cede as many risks as possible, and tap reinsurance much more than outside finance. Conversely, this information-based theory suggests that reinsurance is a costly source of funds, because expertise and monitoring efforts have to be rewarded. As a result, it suggests that primary insurers should try to minimize their cessions. They should restrict cessions to the level at which certification by reinsurers is credible because they are sufficiently exposed. This is consistent with empirical cessions rates of only 14%, and no more than 3% or 4% for large insurance groups.

7.2 Reinsurance and Prudential Supervision

This information-based theory of reinsurance has important implications for insurance regulation. Reinsurers are highly sophisticated monitors of the operations of insurance companies. They are credible monitors too, because their profitability is at stake. Thus, the way that the reinsurance market treats an insurance company should tell the regulator a lot about the company.

An implication of this role of reinsurers as monitors of primary insurers is that prudential supervision should include the collection of detailed information on the structure and pricing of the reinsurance treaties underwritten by insurance companies. The supervisory authorities should develop sufficient expertise to analyze, in a timely fashion, the evolution of reinsurance prices and quantities at the firm and market levels.

This parallels the proposals by Calomiris (1998) and Bliss (2001) to use spreads on subordinated debt to extract market information on banks' solvency. Extracting information from signals sent by the reinsurance market has two advantages over merely observing stock prices.

(1) Like prudential regulators, reinsurers are mainly concerned by extreme losses and the occurrence of very adverse situations. Thus, reinsurance prices, especially in the case of nonproportional reinsurance, send a "pure" signal on downside risk which is not scrambled by the pricing of upside risk. As already mentioned, this was the main argument put forward by proponents of the use of subordinated spreads to assess the solvency of banks.

(2) Moreover, the reinsurance market sends a signal on the risk profile of the insurance portfolio of ceding companies. It is very helpful to have such a pure signal, which disentangles insurance operations from other sources of risk. This is because an insurance company which has fundamentally profitable insurance operations but has experienced losses on, say, a high-yield bond portfolio requires corrective measures that differ dramatically from the ones that should be applied to a company whose insurance operations generate persistent losses.

8

How Does Insurance Regulation Fit within Other Financial Regulations?

This chapter examines how the prudential regulation of insurance fits within other financial regulations—the regulation of banks and financial conglomerates, and the management of systemic risk.

8.1   Insurance and Financial Conglomerates

Prudential regulators should be equipped with specific tools for dealing with financial conglomerates. By conglomerate, we mean a group of firms operating in heterogeneous business lines, the heterogeneity being either geographical or operational (e.g., life and non-life insurance, or insurance and banking). These firms have financial links to each other and are controlled by the same top management and/or shareholders. The number of such conglomerates grew during the 1990s, due to the development of global groups and to a wave of cross-industry mergers within the financial-services industry. Such mergers were motivated by the presumption that it was a good idea to exploit a distribution network as intensively as possible by offering a whole range of financial services to acquired customers. This wave was facilitated in the United States by the

1999 Gramm–Leach–Bliley Act, which dismantled the 1933 Glass–Steagall Act that had made conglomeration illegal. As illustrated by the GAN and Europavie cases, conglomerates are particularly difficult to deal with from a prudential standpoint. There are three main reasons for this. First, their monitoring is made difficult by the opaqueness of their accounts. This is particularly true if they are supervised by several authorities that are from different countries and/or are in charge of different industries. Coordinating these authorities so that at least one of them gets all the relevant information and analyzes it with the relevant expertise may be impossible or at least come at a significant cost. Note that, interestingly, one of the main justifications for the merging of several financial regulators into a single authority in the United Kingdom, Japan, Australia, and Germany was precisely the rise of financial conglomerates within these countries. A second, related reason is that financially distressed conglomerates have the ability to transfer assets secretly and quickly from one entity to the other so that they end up in shareholders' pockets instead of backing insurance liabilities. The third reason is multiple gearing: namely, the fact that the capital of each subsidiary is actually exposed to the risks hosted by the other entities via the internal capital structure. Of course, this pooling of risks and capital also has an upside, namely diversification. This is one of the good reasons why there are conglomerates. Let us study in more detail the interplay between these two competing effects—double gearing and diversification—with the following simple model. First, let us consider the benchmark case of a single insurance company (which we call firm 1) with the following balance sheet:

| Assets A_1 | Reserves R_1 |
| | Equity E_1 |

We denote by $1 + \tilde{x}_1$ the (stochastic) loss ratio, i.e., the ratio of claims over reserves. Normalizing the risk-free rate to zero for simplicity, the return on equity $\tilde{\rho}_1$ is

$$\tilde{\rho}_1 = \frac{A_1 - R_1(1 + \tilde{x}_1)}{E_1} - 1.$$

or

$$\tilde{\rho}_1 = -\frac{R_1}{E_1}\tilde{x}_1.$$

The gearing factor, namely the ratio of financial profitability (return on equity) over operational profitability $\tilde{x}_1$, is the inverse of the solvency margin E_1/R_1. For plausible values of this margin (less than 10%), the gearing factor is typically larger than 10 in insurance companies. Now, in order to generate a simple modeling of an insurance group, let us assume that firm 1 owns the shares of another insurance company, which we call firm 2. For the sake of comparison, we keep the total assets of firm 1 constant. The balance sheets of the two firms are as follows:

Firm 1	
Investment in firm 2 E_2	Reserves R_1
Other Assets $A_1 - E_2$	Equity E_1

Firm 2	
	Reserves R_2
Assets A_2	Equity E_2

The balance sheet for the insurance group as a whole is as follows:

	Reserves $R_1 + R_2$
Assets $A_1 + A_2 - E_2$	Equity E_1

Let $1 + \tilde{x}_1$ and $1 + \tilde{x}_2$ denote the loss-to-reserves ratios of the two firms.

The return on equity of firm 2 is

$$\tilde{\rho}_2 = \frac{A_2 - R_2(1 + \tilde{x}_2)}{E_2} = -\frac{R_2}{E_2}\tilde{x}_2$$

and that of firm 1 is

$$\tilde{\rho}_1 = \frac{A_1 + E_2\tilde{\rho}_2 - R_1(1 + \tilde{x}_1)}{E_1} - 1.$$

Replacing $\tilde{\rho}_2$ by its value and simplifying, we obtain

$$\tilde{\rho}_1 = -\frac{R_1}{E_1}\tilde{x}_1 - \frac{R_2}{E_1}\tilde{x}_2,$$

which can also be written as follows:

$$\tilde{\rho}_1 = \underbrace{-\frac{R_1}{E_1}\tilde{x}_1}_{\text{gearing factor}} - \underbrace{\alpha\left(\frac{R_1}{E_1}\right)\left(\frac{R_2}{E_2}\right)\tilde{x}_2}_{\text{double gearing}},$$

where $\alpha = E_2/R_1$ denotes the exposure of the policyholders of firm 1 to the risks of firm 2.

Now, is the probability of ruin of firm 1 increased or decreased by the acquisition of firm 2? The answer to this question is complex. Assume that both firms are subject to a capital requirement m which they meet exactly,

$$\frac{E_1}{R_1} = \frac{E_2}{R_2} = m,$$

and that $\tilde{x}_1$ and $\tilde{x}_2$ have a joint distribution with mean $\binom{0}{0}$ and covariance matrix

$$\begin{pmatrix} \sigma_x^2 & \nu \\ \nu & \sigma_x^2 \end{pmatrix}.$$

Then $\tilde{\rho}_1$ is also normally distributed with zero mean and has a variance σ^2 given by

$$\sigma^2 = \frac{\sigma_x^2}{m^2}\left(1 + 2\frac{\alpha}{m}\nu + \frac{\alpha^2}{m^2}\right).$$

Prior to the acquisition of firm 2, the variance of the return on equity (ROE) of firm 1 was σ_x^2/m^2. After the acquisition of firm 2, the variance of the ROE of firm 1 (and thus its probability of ruin) becomes σ^2. The above formula shows that $\sigma^2 > \sigma_x^2/m^2$ if and only if

$$\nu > -\frac{\alpha}{2m}.$$

When the risks of both companies are positively correlated (no diversification), i.e., when $\nu \geqslant 0$, or when the acquisition is large in relation to the capitalization of firm 1 (i.e., when α/m is sufficiently large), the risk of failure of firm 1 increases. This is because of double gearing. Notice, however, that the above inequality shows that when diversification is important (ν close to -1) and α/m is small (small acquisition) the probability of ruin of firm 1 may be decreased after the acquisition.

Before outlining our recommendations regarding the regulation of conglomerates, let us use this simple model to evaluate the "solo-plus" rule advocated by "Solvency II," a new project of directives on insurance supervision initiated by the European Commission. The Commission acknowledges that there is something special about conglomerates. The "solo-plus" rule means that each insurance subsidiary must meet capital requirements, and that the group as a whole must also meet them based on the consolidated accounts.[1] This is a straightforward, but very conservative, way of accounting for double gearing. In our simple example, the solo-plus rule means that an additional solvency requirement is introduced:

$$E_1 \geqslant (R_1 + R_2)m.$$

Recall that the return on equity of firm 1 can be written as

$$\tilde{\rho}_1 = -\frac{R_1\tilde{x}_1 + R_2\tilde{x}_2}{E_1}.$$

---

[1] The consolidated capital requirements would be a hybrid formula when the group does banking and insurance.

As a result, the solo-plus rule turns out to be very conservative. It ensures indeed that even if the operations of firm 1 and firm 2 are perfectly positively correlated, for example, if $\tilde{x}_1 = \tilde{x}_2 = \tilde{x}$, then the probability of ruin of the conglomerate is not larger than that of isolated companies. Ruin only occurs, in fact, if

$$\tilde{x} \leqslant -\frac{E_1}{R_1 + R_2} = -m.$$

If, more realistically, the correlation is smaller than 1, solo-plus targets reduce the probability of ruin. Conglomerates are thus treated unfairly with respect to isolated companies. To avoid this "uneven" playing field, the capital requirement formula has to be changed. The correct formula is the following RBC-type formula:

$$E_1 \geqslant m\sqrt{R_1^2 + R_2^2 + 2\rho R_1 R_2}$$

It is undoubtedly reasonable to assume that risks within a conglomerate are not completely independent. As problems arise in one part of the group, they are likely to spread within the group because they distort the incentives of management and shareholders. Moreover, the opaqueness of conglomerates may also justify the regulator being more conservative and imposing tighter solvency requirements. Higher capital requirements provide the supervisor with more time to figure out what is really going on before it is too late. However, the solo-plus rule sounds overly conservative. This rule does not take into account any possible benefit from diversification within conglomerates. A more lenient rule based on an estimate of ρ seems theoretically desirable, but is hardly applicable in practice. Estimating ρ is too difficult, because ρ depends on the details of the organization of the group, and particularly on the degree of integration of its operations.

Our "double-trigger" structure can be adapted to conglomerates so as to account for both the risk of higher opaqueness and double gearing and for the benefits from diversification. The broad idea is that the first trigger should be tougher and the second more lenient. Remember that the role of the first threshold is to trigger mandatory investigations by the regulator. Such investigations should be triggered either if one of the insurance companies within the group does not satisfy the first threshold on a "solo" basis, or if the group does not satisfy the consolidated ratio based on the group's consolidated accounts. This consolidated capital requirement should be more demanding than the "solo" one applied to consolidated accounts. This accounts for the fact that conglomerates are opaque, so that more attention must be devoted to assessing their actual economic situation. This also deals with the fact that, as part of a conglomerate, a firm is subject to the risk of having its assets used to bail out another entity of the group, or that it may participate in a gambling-for-resurrection strategy triggered by problems somewhere else in the group. However, the second threshold, the one which starts the liquidation process, i.e., grants full control rights to the regulator and the guarantee fund, should be lower for an entity within a group than for an isolated firm. There are several reasons for this. One is better liquidity: a firm within a group is less vulnerable to liquidity shocks than an isolated firm. Another is corporate governance. If properly monitored, the conglomerate may indeed have strong incentives to restructure itself in an orderly fashion without taking too much risk in order to preserve the well-performing part of the conglomerate. Moreover, the scrap value of a conglomerate is in general larger than the sum of each entity's liquidation value. The conglomerate may indeed be sold piece by piece, and some goodwill may be pocketed by the entities which are still performing well and thus sold as going concerns. Figure 8.1 illustrates this adaptation of our "double-trigger" supervision to the supervision of conglomerates.

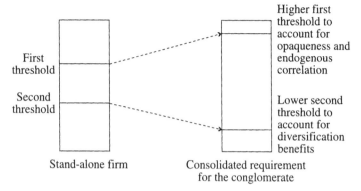

Figure 8.1. "Double-trigger" supervision
in the case of conglomerates.

8.2 The Regulation of Banks and of Insurance Companies Are Two Different Jobs

There are two major differences between the scenario of financial distress for a bank and that for an insurance company: liquidity problems and systemic risk.

Contrary to what happens for insurance companies, financial distress for banks almost immediately translates into liquidity problems: indeed, a large part of a bank's liabilities consists of demandable deposits, which are likely to be withdrawn in great numbers as soon as depositors anticipate some problem (this is the historical form of a "bank run"). The same is true of overnight loans that counterparties refuse to renew at the slightest signal of financial distress (this is the modern form of a "bank run"). This has justified the introduction of "emergency liquidity assistance" facilities by central banks (this is the "lender of last resort" activity, which was introduced by the Bank of England in 1890 during the first Barings crisis and which was later adopted by most central banks) as well as, more recently, deposit insurance systems. In spite of these sophisticated prudential regulation systems, many countries (especially but not exclusively emerging countries) have recently experienced spectacular banking crises. A good account of these crises can be found in, for example, Lindgren et al. (1996). Some economists (see, for example, Detragiache and Demirgüç-Kunt 1997) have argued that financial-safety-net systems (particularly deposit insurance funds) were actually responsible for these crises, because they generate moral hazard in bankers' behavior. The difficulty is that these systems are often under the control of governments and they are sometimes misused for political reasons: in order to bail out insolvent banks that should have been closed.

A second distinctive feature of banks (as opposed to insurance companies) is that they tend to fail in clusters, either because their assets are highly sensitive to macroeconomic shocks that simultaneously hit all the banks in a country (recessions, stock exchange or real-estate crashes) or because individual bank failures propagate to the rest of the banks. This feature, known as systemic risk, has often been used by governments to justify bailouts of insolvent banks (e.g., Continental Illinois in 1984 in the United States).

Although the topic is still debated in the academic literature (see Bhattacharya et al. (2004), Freixas and Rochet (1995), and Santos (2000) for extended surveys), a large consensus seems to have emerged on the rationale behind such government bailouts in the banking sector. It is now widely accepted that bank regulation and supervision have essentially two purposes.

(1) To protect small depositors, by limiting the frequency and cost of individual bank failures. This is often referred to as micro-prudential policy.

(2) To protect the banking system as a whole, by limiting the frequency and cost of systemic banking crises. This is often referred to as macro-prudential policy.

Empirical evidence suggests that liquidity risk is negligible in the insurance sector. Due to the different maturity structure of insurers' balance sheets, insurance companies are not typically subject to liquidity problems, even when they are financially distressed. In more-financial language, bank equity has a highly positive duration and convexity, while insurance equity has low or even negative duration and low convexity. Moreover, as we explain in more detail in the next section, there does not seem to be any evidence in favor of contagion of failures in insurance. The only detailed empirical analysis we are aware of is provided by Polonchek and Miller (1999), who study the impact of the announcement of new capital issuance by an insurance company. Such an announcement generally has a negative impact on the stock price of the company in question (it is considered to be "bad news" by financial analysts, since firms typically prefer to issue debt; only the firms that have not been able to issue debt will issue equity). In the banking sector, such an announcement also has a negative impact on the stock price of *other* banks, which has to be interpreted as evidence of contagion: if a bank is in financial distress, it is likely that other banks will also be hurt, either because they have invested in similar assets or because they are financially linked to the first bank. In the case of insurance companies, Polonchek and Miller (1999) find no evidence for such contagion in property liability. They cannot statistically reject the possibility of some contagion effect in the life-insurance sector, but find that the economic magnitude of this effect is very small.

As a result, there is not a strong case for government intervention in the supervision of insurance companies, as there is for banks. Given the time-consistency problem faced by governments (coming from the fact that it is difficult for them to commit in advance not to bail out insolvent institutions), granting insurance supervisory authorities independence from political pressure would clearly constitute an improvement over the situation in which this is not the case.

To summarize, we believe that the arguments in favor of soft regulation in banking—liquidity risk and systemic risk—are much less convincing in the insurance industry. The regulator should therefore be much closer in nature to the tough claimholder suggested by the "representation hypothesis" of Dewatripont and Tirole (1994) in the insurance industry than in banking.

8.3 Insurance and Systemic Risk

In this section, we would like to comment on the few and well-identified potential sources of systemic risk in the insurance industry. Let us first make clear what we mean by systemic risk.

What Is Systemic Risk?

A systemic risk is a source of uncertainty that simultaneously and significantly affects most firms within one large industry or geographical area. As already mentioned, such risks are a first-order concern in banking, because banks' borrowers may be symmetrically and simultaneously affected by macroeconomic or financial shocks. These aggregate shocks may be amplified by the response of the financial system. If each bank responds to a small degradation of the solvency of its borrowers by tightening its credit policy or collateral requirements in order to preserve its prudential ratios, the aggregate outcome is a withdrawal of liquidity from the economy. This may make the situation of the borrowers worse, thereby increasing their probabilities of default. This feedback between an *exogenous* shock and the *endogenous* response of the financial sector may greatly amplify an initial shock and ultimately create a banking "panic" in which liquidity dries up and most banks become insolvent. In other words, individual banks fail to internalize the fact that risk-management policies that seem rational at the firm level may lead to an increase in aggregate risk.

Systemic risk is an important concern for financial institutions only because of the possibility of such feedback mechanisms. There are not many historical examples of purely *exogenous* shocks bringing down the financial system.[2] Harmful systemic risks, such as stock market crashes or bank panics, generally involve both an exogenous shock and an endogenous response of the financial system that amplify each other. Prudential regulations at the firm level are usually responsible for causing such feedback loops to develop. For instance, there is a large consensus that portfolio insurance programs, selling mechanically when stock prices fall, played an important role in the U.S. stock market crash of 1987 (Brady 1988). Also, the Basel II reform toward more risk-based capital requirements for banks has provoked fierce debate on its possible destabilizing consequences (Danielsson et al. 2001). Thus, in the presence of endogenous risk, an excessive focus of prudential regulation on risk management at the firm level may destabilize the whole insurance industry by amplification of exogenous shocks. This is the sense in which systemic risk matters. Systemic risk is significant in practice only in the presence of a possible endogenous feedback. But is such an endogenous risk important in insurance?

Does Endogenous Risk Exist in Insurance?

Insurance companies collect premiums against the promise of the future indemnization of losses. Thus, they are subject to two types of risk:

- the occurrence and magnitude of the losses are uncertain—this is technical risk;

---

[2] Of course, we rule out major historical events such as acts of war or major political crises, which bring down whole social institutions.

- the rate of return earned on the investment of premiums until claims are settled is unknown—this is financial risk.

One reason why insurance panics are rare is that technical risk has no chance of being significantly amplified by the insurance industry. As detailed in Danielsson and Shin (2003), endogenous risk exists when financial institutions play games against each other: for instance, when hedge funds speculate in the same market. In this case, their actions are based on their beliefs about the actions of the others, which may yield self-fulfilling prophecies. But in the case of technical risk, insurance companies play only against nature or courts. The large, worldwide diversification, as well as the intertemporal smoothing performed by the reinsurance market, suffice to control purely exogenous shocks.

Financial risk, however, is the quintessential endogenous risk. For instance, if interest rates decrease, life-insurance companies, whose equity has a negative duration, need to buy large quantities of bonds to match their rapidly increasing liabilities, which may further boost bonds' prices if the whole insurance market has granted overly generous long-term interest rate guarantees. Our view on prudential regulation needs to be partly amended to accommodate this endogenous risk. For instance, the British Financial Services Authority has softened the stress-test requirements after 9/11 to avoid fire sales of stocks by life-insurance companies, which would have further depressed stock markets that were already in turmoil.

More generally, given that insurance companies are major institutional investors, it seems desirable to modify capital requirements after the occurrence of very severe shocks on interest rates or on an important class of assets such as stocks or real estate, in order to avoid systemic risk. More precisely, the rules must be sufficiently well-indexed on market conditions that the rules themselves do not influence markets. However, in our example of falling interest rates, the firms that have granted the most unreasonable guarantees to the policyholders should be punished *ex post* by having their portfolios transferred to the more reasonable firms. In other words, an amendment to our view of prudential regulation is that it should be tough on idiosyncratic risks and insurance risks, but it should be soft on systematic, market-wide financial risks.

9

Conclusion: Prudential Regulation as a Substitute for Corporate Governance

Because the customers of insurance companies, that is, policyholders, are their main creditors, their interests should be protected in the very same way as the main creditors of other firms—typically, sophisticated financial institutions such as banks—have their interests protected. Unlike in sophisticated financial institutions, policyholders are dispersed, often-uninformed claimholders, and do not necessarily have the skills to monitor their insurer. This is why the monitoring task is typically delegated to a specific institution: the supervisory authority. The main challenge, when designing the prudential regulation system, is to make this delegation as efficient as possible. Namely, the regulator must have the appropriate tools and incentives to act as the "banker" of insurers.

This point may sound obvious, but it has deep practical consequences on the design of a prudential authority. Some practitioners have in mind that a prudential regulator, as a public authority, should be a moderator, reconciling the interests of current and future policyholders, shareholders, and the workforce through gentle but ongoing and pervasive interventions. *In our view, an efficient regulatory action is the exact opposite.* The only convincing raison d'être of prudential regulation is the policyholders' coordination problem. As long as an insurance company does well, it is optimal to let the top management and shareholders run it without constraints. There is no reason an external authority should interfere—it is very unlikely to be more skilled than them, and managerial entrepreneurial spirit is exactly what all the claimholders, including policyholders, need. Conversely, if the firm becomes undercapitalized, the prudential authority must intervene in a prompt and tough fashion, focusing only and pigheadedly on current policyholders' interests. Its aim must be to maximize the recovery value of their claims, regardless of the cost to the management, workforce, and shareholders. This clear rule for regulatory intervention, though apparently too tough in bad times and too lenient in good times, is the efficient one. It ensures *ex ante* that insurance companies make the right decision at the right time. Thus, it maximizes the social value of insurance. Paradoxically, it is difficult in practice to set up a public authority which fulfills such a simple but focused task satisfactorily. By nature, such organizations tend to act more smoothly, and consider the overall social and political consequences of their decisions before acting. Public regulators might aim to expand the scope of their mission in order to increase their resources. We have tried to offer recommendations for the design of insurance supervision that help to overcome this bias.

References

Aghion, P., and P. Bolton. 1992. An incomplete contracts approach to financial contracting. *Review of Economic Studies* 59:473–94.

Arrow, K. 1963. Uncertainty and the welfare economics of medical care. *American Economic Review* 53:941–73.

Bhattacharya, S., A. W. Boot, and A. Thakor (eds). 2004. *Credit, Intermediation and the Macroeconomy.* Oxford University Press.

Blake, D. 2001. An assessment of the adequacy and objectivity of the information provided by the board of the Equitable Life Assurance Society in connection with the compromise scheme proposal of 6 December 2001. Pensions Institute Report (available at www.pensions-institute.org/reports/equitablelife_DBreport.pdf).

Bliss, R. R. 2001. Market discipline and subordinated debt: a review of some salient issues. *Economic Perspectives, Federal Reserve Bank of Chicago* 1:24–45.

Brady, N. 1988. *Report of the Presidential Task Force on Market Mechanisms.* Washington, DC: Government Printing Office.

Calomiris, C. W. 1998. Blueprints for a new global financial architecture. United States House of Representatives Report (available at www.house.gov/jec/imf/blueprnt.htm).

Cour des Comptes. 2000. L'intervention de l'État dans la crise du secteur financier. Rapport au President de la Republique, Paris (November 2000; available at www.ccomptes.fr/cour-des-comptes / publications / rapports / crisesf / intervention-etat-dans-crise-secteur-financier.pdf).

Cummins, J. D., S. E. Harrington, and R. Klein. 1995. Solvency experience, risk-based capital, and prompt corrective action in property-liability insurance. Center for Financial Institutions Working Paper 95-06, Wharton School Center for Financial Institutions, University of Pennsylvania.

Cummins, J. D., M. F. Grace, and R. D. Phillips. 1999. Regulatory solvency prediction in property-liability insurance: risk-based capital, audit ratios, and cash flow simulation. *Journal of Risk and Insurance* 66(3):417–58.

Danielsson, J., and H. Shin. 2003. Endogenous risk. In *Modern Risk Management: A History*. London: Risk Books.

Danielsson, J., P. Embrechts, C. Goodhart, C. Keating, F. Muennich, O. Renault, and H. Shin. 2001. An academic response to Basel II. Financial Markets Group Special Paper 130 (available at http://hyunsongshin.org/www/basel2.pdf).

Detragiache, E., and A. Demirgüç-Kunt. 1997. The determinants of banking crises—evidence from developing and developed countries. IMF Working Paper 97/106. International Monetary Fund.

Dewatripont, M., and J. Tirole. 1994. *The Prudential Regulation of Banks*. Cambridge, MA: MIT Press.

Doherty, N. A., and K. Smetters. 2005. Moral hazard in reinsurance markets. *Journal of Risk and Insurance* 72(3):375–91.

Freixas, X., and J.-C. Rochet. 1995. *Microeconomics of Banking*. Cambridge, MA: MIT Press.

Garven, J. R., and J. Lamm-Tennant. 2003. The demand for reinsurance: theory and empirical tests. *Insurance and Risk Management* 71(2):217–37.

Grace, M., S. Harrington, and R. Klein. 1993. Risk-based capital standards and insurer insolvency risk: an empirical analysis. Presented at the 1993 Annual Meeting of the American Risk and Insurance Association, San Francisco, CA.

Group of Thirty. 2006. Reinsurance and international financial markets. Group of Thirty Report (available at www.group30.org/pubs.php).

Hart, O. 1988. Incomplete contracts and the theory of the firm. *Journal of Law, Economics and Organization* 4(1):119–39.

———. 1995. *Firms, Contracts, and Financial Structure*. Oxford University Press.

Holmström, B., and J. Tirole. 1997. Financial intermediation, loanable funds and the real sector. *Quarterly Journal of Economics* 112:663–92.

Kim, D., and A. Santomero. 1988. Risk in banking and capital regulation. *Journal of Finance* 43:1219–33.

Lindgren, C., G. Garcia, and M. Seal. 1996. *Bank Soundness and Macroeconomic Policy.* Washington, DC: International Monetary Fund.

Mayers, D., and C. W. Smith Jr. 1990. On the corporate demand for insurance: evidence from the reinsurance market. *Journal of Business* 63(1):19–40.

Modigliani, F., and M. Miller. 1958. The cost of capital, corporate finance and the theory of investment. *American Economic Review* 48:261–97.

Morrison, A. D. 2004. Life insurance: regulation as contract enforcement. *Economic Affairs* 24(4):47–52.

Polonchek, J., and R. K. Miller. 1999. Contagion effects in the insurance industry. *Journal of Risk and Insurance* 66(3):459–75.

Rochet, J. C. 1992. Capital requirements and the behaviour of commercial banks. *European Economic Review* 43:981–90.

Santos, J. A. C. 2000. Bank capital regulation in contemporary banking theory: a review of the literature. BIS Working Paper 90. Bank for International Settlements.

Swiss Re. 1998. The global reinsurance market in the midst of consolidation. *Sigma* 9:3–33.